Mental Skills for Athletes

Mental Skills for Athletes: A Workbook for Competitive Success is a step-by-step guide for developing a toolbox of mental skills. In this user-friendly workbook, Dr. Betsy Shoenfelt compiles materials from over 35 years of experience as a performance psychologist working to achieve competitive excellence, creating the go-to resource for athletes and coaches in any sport and at any level.

The book includes succinct, easily understood explanations of key mental skills based on the science of performance excellence. It discusses both cognitive and physical skills to ensure competitive success, covering a range of topics including focus, confidence, resilience, mindfulness, motivation, role clarity, problem solving, team values, and strategic goal setting. Shoenfelt includes over 25 different exercises to ensure the reader can readily apply these skills across a variety of sports and across all levels of competition, from high school to Olympic athletes. Worksheets encourage a hands-on approach and provide structure to guide the appropriate implementation of mental skills for each athlete. Examples of completed worksheets help demonstrate to the reader how to best utilize these resources.

This book is essential for early career sport psychology practitioners across the globe, as well as aspiring graduate students. The book is an invaluable resource for coaches and athletes at all levels.

Elizabeth L. Shoenfelt, Ph.D., University Distinguished Professor in the Department of Psychological Sciences at Western Kentucky University, USA, is a performance psychologist with 35+ years of experience working in business, industry, government, education, and sports with individuals, teams, and organizations to achieve performance excellence.

Mental Skills for Athletes

A Workbook for Competitive Success

ELIZABETH L. SHOENFELT

For my dear aunt, Kitty Neil.
Thank you for your love and
support!

Live strong, live smart,
First with your head,
Then with your heart. ♡
With much love,
Betsy

Routledge
Taylor & Francis Group

NEW YORK AND LONDON

First published 2019
by Routledge
52 Vanderbilt Avenue, New York, NY 10017

and by Routledge
2 Park Square, Milton Park, Abingdon, Oxon, OX14 4RN

Routledge is an imprint of the Taylor & Francis Group, an informa business

© 2019 Taylor & Francis

Library of Congress Cataloging-in-Publication Data
Names: Shoenfelt, Elizabeth, author.
Title: Mental skills for athletes : a workbook for competitive success / Elizabeth L. Shoenfelt.
Description: New York, NY : Routledge, [2019] | Includes bibliographical references.
Identifiers: LCCN 2018060705 (print) | LCCN 2019005504 (ebook) | ISBN 9780429268694 (Ebook) | ISBN 9780367219116 (hardback) | ISBN 9780367219130 (pbk.) | ISBN 9780429268694 (ebk)
Subjects: LCSH: Sports—Psychological aspects. | Athletes—Psychology. | Athletes—Attitudes.
Classification: LCC GV706.4 (ebook) | LCC GV706.4 .S5236 2019 (print) | DDC 796.01/9—dc23
LC record available at https://lccn.loc.gov/2018060705

ISBN: 978-0-367-21911-6 (hbk)
ISBN: 978-0-367-21913-0 (pbk)
ISBN: 978-0-429-26869-4 (ebk)

Typeset in Bembo
by codeMantra

Contents

Acknowledgments   viii

Part I Introduction   1

1 An Introduction to Mental Skills   3

Part II Mental Skills
A. The Mind (Cognitive Skills)   7

2 Positive Self-Talk, Confidence, and Focus   9
Mental Skills: Self-Talk – The Power of Positive Thinking 9
Mental Skills: Use Positive Self-Talk to Build Confidence 10
Mental Skills: Focus on the "3 Ps" 11
Mental Skills: Focus – More than the "3 Ps" 13
Key Concepts for Positive Self-Talk, Confidence, and Focus 14

   Exercises and Techniques   15
   Exercise 2.1: Changing Negative Self-Talk to Positive Self-Talk 16
   Exercise 2.2: Self-Talk Journal 17
   Exercise 2.3: Self-Talk Exercise – Reflect and Reconstruct 19
   Exercise 2.4: Self-Talk – Anticipate Situations 21
   Exercise 2.5: Self-Talk Tracking and Affirmation Statements for Focus Areas 23
   Exercise 2.6: Post Your Focus Areas and Affirmation Statements 31
   Exercise 2.7: Identify Types of Appropriate and Inappropriate Focus 33
   Exercise 2.8: Focus Technique – Putting Distractions on Hold 35
   Exercise 2.9: Focusing Through Distractions 37
      Exercise 2.9a: 30-Second Focus 37
      Exercise 2.9b: Changing Channels 37

3 Motivation   38
Theories of Motivation 38
Mental Skills: Goal Setting 40
Key Concepts for Motivation 41

Exercises and Techniques   42
   Exercise 3.1: Setting Goals   43
   Exercise 3.2: A Checklist to Ensure Effective Goals   47
   Exercise 3.3: Examples of Techniques to Track Performance Relative to
      Goals to Provide Feedback   48
   Exercise 3.4: The Goal Setting–Satisfaction Paradox   51

4 Imagery   55
   Mental Skills: Imagery for Performance Enhancement 55
   Key Concepts for Imagery 56

   Exercises and Techniques   57
      Exercise 4.1: The Imagery Rating Scale 58
      Exercise 4.2: Images for Basic Senses 64
      Exercise 4.3: Sport-Specific Images 65
      Exercise 4.4: Fun with Imagery 68
      Exercise 4.5: Using Imagery to Successfully Deal with Problem Situations 70

5 Problem Solving and Continuous Learning to Build Resilience 72
   Mental Skills: Error-Based Learning 73
   Key Concepts for Problem Solving and Continuous Learning 74

   Exercises and Techniques   74
      Exercise 5.1: Review and Reflect for Continuous Learning 75
      Exercise 5.2: Dealing with the "What Ifs" 79

Part II   Mental Skills   **83**
       B. The Body (Physiological Skills and the Mind–Body Connection)

6 Relaxation, Controlling Performance Anxiety, and Mindfulness   85
   Mental Skills: Relaxation and Control of Physiological Arousal 85
   Mental Skills: Mindfulness 87
   Key Concepts in Relaxation, Controlling Performance Anxiety, and
      Mindfulness 87

   Exercises and Techniques   89
      Exercise 6.1: Deep Breathing to Release Tension and Relax 89
      Exercise 6.2: Tracking Your Relaxation 90
         Preparing for a Relaxation Session 90
         Pre-Relaxation Questionnaire 91
         Post-Relaxation Questionnaire 92
      Exercise 6.3: Mindfulness of Our Senses 93
         Exercise 6.3a: Mindfully Experience a Raisin 94
      Exercise 6.4: Other Brief Mindfulness Exercises 95
         Make the Old New Again 95
         Attentive Listening 95

7 Automaticity and Practice   96
   Mental Skills: Automaticity 96
   Mental Skills: Perfect Practice Makes Perfect 98
   Key Concepts in Automaticity and Practice 99

8 Routines   101
   Mental Skills: Using a Performance Routine 101
   Practice 102

Superstitions 103
Key Concepts in Routines 103
Examples of Routines for Different Sports 104
Example 8.1: Golf Swing Routine 105
Example 8.2: Volleyball Serve Routine 107
Example 8.3: Basketball Free Throw Routine 108
Example 8.4: Baseball Pitching Routine 109
Develop Your Own Routine – Example with Punting in Football 110

Part III   Team Skills and Special Situations   **111**

9 Role Clarity for Team Sports   113
   A Structured Process for Increasing Role Clarity in Team Sports 114
   Example of a Role Grid for Basketball 116
   Example of a Role Grid Completed by Dominique 117
   Team Role Perception Feedback Sheet for Dominique 121
   Team Role Perception Feedback Sheet for Alex 122
   Team Role Perceptions Feedback Sheet for Jordan 123
   How Effective is the Role Process? 125

10 The Importance of Team Values   127
   Exercise to Identify Team Values 129
   Individual "Team Values" 129
   Combining Individual "Team Values" 130
   Prioritize Team Values 131

11 Strategic Goal Setting for Teams   132
   A Strategic Team Goal-Setting Process 132
   Outcomes from Strategic Goal Setting 133
   Example of Strategic Goal Setting with an Intercollegiate
   *   Volleyball Team 133*
   Conclusion 135

12 Preparing for the Big Event   136
   Maintaining Motivation: Staying Strong through the Mid-Season Drudgery 136
   Exercise 12.1: Work Today to Achieve Your Dream 137
   Mental Skills: Pre-Competition Routine 138
   Mental Skills: The (Distracting) Role of Context 139
   Exercise 12.2: Setting Aside Distractions 140
   Mental Skills: The Four Pillars of Confidence 140
   Exercise 12.3: Building Confidence 143
   Summary Sheets 144

   Additional Exercises and Techniques   147
   (Team) Exercise 12.4: Singing the Star Spangled Banner 148
   Lessons Learned: What are the "Take Aways" from this Exercise? 149
   Exercise 12.5: Develop the Mindset of a Champion 150
   Example of Developing the Mindset of a Champion 151

Part IV   Epilogue   **153**

Index   157

Acknowledgments

For almost 40 years, I have been fortunate to work with great coaches and athletes who welcomed me into their locker rooms and their courts/fields/pools/gyms. These discerning coaches invited me into their teams of professionals to use the science of performance excellence and sport psychology to help develop their athletes into top performers who, in toto, have won numerous conference championships and NCAA tournament games, received All American honors, and even an Olympic gold medal. To these coaches and athletes, I express my gratitude and my admiration. I also want to express my appreciation to my personal support team Nike, Annie, and Lily, who truly exemplify positivity as only canines can.

Part I

Introduction

An Introduction to Mental Skills

1

Welcome to *Mental Skills for Athletes: A Workbook for Competitive Success*! As a performance psychologist, I frequently hear statements such as:

- "I want my athletes to be mentally tough."
- "Can you help me work on my mental game?"
- "I need to get out of my head."
- "Golf is 90% mental."

All of these statements reflect a recognition that there is an important mental component to athletic performance. Mental skills give you an edge in competition. When two teams or two athletes equal in skill and ability compete, the mentally tough one wins virtually every time. When an underdog overcomes a more talented opponent, it likely can be attributed to focus, intensity, and tenacity; that is, mental skills.

Although some may believe that 90% of performance is mental, that is not the case. If you are an athlete performing at a high level such as intercollegiate or as a pro, in reality, mental skills can improve your "game" by about 10%. Performing at a high level requires a combination of ability, proper technique and mechanics, strategy, a lot of practice/training, and, yes, mental skills. The 10% improvement in performance that can be accomplished with mental skills means a golfer shooting 80 can improve his game to the low 70s; a swimmer clocking a 75 second 100 meter butterfly can cut her time to 68 seconds; a batter hitting .250 can improve to .275, a basketball player shooting 68% from the free throw line can improve to 75%. In virtually every sport, a 10% improvement is significant. Athletes at all levels can improve their performance by using mental skills. Accomplished athletes with sound technique and mechanics, good strategy, and a strong work ethic can move to the top of their sport. Beginner, intermediate, or advanced intermediate performers can achieve the 10% improvement with mental skills, but also need to attend to mechanics and strategy. These athletes should work closely with a coach – just as elite athletes do. Deliberate practice in which an athlete has guidance and feedback from a sport specific coach(es) and the willingness to practice over the long haul is prerequisite for mental skills to enhance performance.

This workbook will help you develop a toolbox of mental skills based on the science of performance excellence. You will learn cognitive (thinking) skills as well as physical (doing) skills. In any competitive situation, it is important to pull out the appropriate tools/mental skills for performance success. Sport psychologists speak of the mind–body connection. As you will learn, this important connection means that the mind influences the body and the body influences the mind. We need to learn how to control this influence so that we can optimize performance.

Control is the essence of mental skills. In a competitive situation, there are many things we cannot control. We cannot control the referees or umpires, whether we are competing at home or away, the weather, the fans, the competition, your coach, etc., etc. Mentally tough athletes control the controllables – the things you can control or influence. The one thing you should always be able to control is yourself – **how you respond to the situation**. Mental skills enable us to choose how we respond in even the most stressful situation. When you are not in control of your response, you enable your competition, the situation, the referees, etc. to control you. When you are in control, you determine how you respond. You may choose to respond in a calm manner or you may choose to respond with a high energy response. The important thing is that you, not something or someone else in the situation, determine how you respond. Mental skills enable you to be in control of your response in any high demand, competitive situation. Staying in control and responding with pride, determination, and resilience is the essence of mental toughness. It should be noted that along with personal control comes personal responsibility and accountability. That is, you are responsible for your response – behaviorally and mentally, even in a tough, challenging situation.

Mental skills, just like other performance skills, require practice. This workbook provides succinct descriptions of key mental skills for individual and team performance. This workbook also provides worksheets that, in essence, are homework that will enable you to practice the mental skills you will be learning and to track your improvement using each mental skill. It is important to practice each of the mental skills you wish to add to your toolbox. You would never attempt to dribble a basketball, swing a golf club, pass a football, hit a baseball, serve a volleyball, or execute any specific skill in competition without many hours of practice. Likewise, for mental skills to be optimally effective in improving your performance in competition, you must practice using them. I recommend that you keep all of your mental skills worksheets in a binder or, if you are an electronics fan, in a well-labeled folder on your computer. Retaining and reviewing your worksheets will allow you to see the gradual progress you make over time.

The first major section of this workbook (Part II, A) focuses on The Mind, or cognitive skills. These are the mental skills that involve thinking and using our head to enhance our performance. As you will learn, what we tell ourselves about a situation and our ability to perform effectively in that situation greatly influence our performance, either in a negative way or a positive way. Cognitive skills help to ensure your thoughts and perceptions have a positive impact on your performance; these skills are essential in developing resilience. First we will address positive self-talk, probably the most foundational of all mental skills. Positive self-talk naturally combines with focus and confidence, so these skills are addressed together. Second, you will learn the skill of goal setting, a straightforward technique that, when done properly, will direct your efforts and improve your performance. Imagery or visualization is another important cognitive skill many athletes find helpful. The final cognitive skill we will address is problem solving. That is, how do you combine the various skills in your mental skills toolbox to deal with challenges or the unexpected? Experience tells us there will be challenges when competing. Learning to expect the unexpected and developing the resilience to deal effectively with each challenge will make success more likely.

The second major section of this workbook (Part II, B) focuses on The Body, or physiological skills and the mind-body connection. First, you will learn to control your physiological response by learning relaxation techniques that, when paired with positive self-talk, enable you to control performance anxiety. Then we address the important role of automaticity, a motor-learning based phenomenon that optimizes our performance when we are fatigued or stressed and helps make our performance more efficient and effective. Automaticity underlies routines (e.g., shot routine in golf or free-throw routine in basketball) and is the reason repetition is such an important component of practice.

The final major section of this workbook (Part III) deals with Team Skills and Special Situations. First, a structured technique for clarifying roles for individual team members is provided. Identifying team values and strategic team goal setting are addressed next. Finally, we will revisit confidence for the big event and how to deal with the distracting role of context.

In each chapter in this workbook, you will be presented with a short, but precise explanation of a mental skill, an example of how successful athletes have implemented the skill to improve their performance, and worksheets to direct your efforts and to track your progress in developing the skill. It is likely that all mental skills in this workbook will not be equally attractive or useful for your particular situation. However, identifying the relevant mental skills and working to develop them and implement them in competition is sure to improve your performance. Developing an array of mental skills will provide you with the tools needed for mental toughness in difficult competitive situations. With this workbook, you will learn a number of mental skills to keep in your mental toughness toolbox. Remember that mental skills require practice – just as any skill does. It is up to you to practice these skills until you are comfortable with them so that you can pull them out and use them when the going gets tough in competitive situations.

Part II

Mental Skills

A. The Mind (Cognitive Skills)

Positive Self-Talk, Confidence, and Focus

2

The first mental skill we address is Positive Self-Talk, likely the most foundational of all mental skills. Being positive involves intentionally stopping negative self-talk and replacing it with positive self-talk, using positive self-talk to build confidence, and focusing on the controllables – those aspects of the situation we can impact. These three mental skills of positive self-talk, confidence, and focus are so interrelated, they are presented together.

Mental Skills: Self-Talk – The Power of Positive Thinking

We constantly talk to ourselves, whether we realize it or not. Most of us don't do this out loud, but we are continually thinking and evaluating. What we tell ourselves about a situation is called "Self-Talk" and is a very important influence on our behavior. *Positive* self-talk is key for successful athletes. Positive self-talk leads to confidence. Winners tell themselves "I can do it. I can prevail in this situation." We need to learn to replace negative self-talk with positive self-talk to develop confidence.

What do you tell yourself in a tough situation in competition? Do you think – "This is awful; I can't stand this; I will never be able to hit the ball; this just isn't fair; I am such a loser to have hit that shot."? These are examples of negative self-talk. Negative self-talk stems from: (a) *awfulizing* – thinking in terms of how bad or tragic the situation is; that you cannot tolerate the situation; (b) thinking in terms of *absolutes* – always/never, total failure/complete success rather in terms of degrees; or (c) *condemnation* of others (or yourself). Negative self-talk prevents you from being effective. Even though responding with negative self-talk in difficult situations is human nature, it is not rational or realistic and causes an athlete to doubt his/her ability, which leads to tentative performance, which leads to more poor performance, which leads to further self-doubt. This progression is called the "downward spiral." To stop and reverse the downward spiral, an athlete must stop negative self-talk and replace it with positive self-talk.

Positive self-talk focuses on what you can do, what is right about the situation. Positive self-talk recognizes that there are issues and challenges, but focuses on the best-case outcome in a difficult situation. Tell yourself – "This is a difficult shot, but I can make it. I prefer not to compete at this site, but I can deal with it. This is not fair, but life is not fair and I can handle it."

To gain perspective, ask yourself, "What is the most awful thing I can imagine happening?" [Stop and really think of the most awful thing that could happen in your life right now.] What did you think of? Most people think of a tragic accident where a loved one is hurt or killed. That is truly an awful event. Now, ask yourself, "If that is 100% bad, then how would I rate missing the shot, hitting a ball out of bounds, losing a point, even losing a game?" It doesn't even compare. Unfortunately, we may encounter some truly awful situations in our lives. Even our worst performance in competition is not that awful compared to a truly awful event.

Save awfulizing for truly awful events. When talking to yourself about a tough situation, replace emotionally hot words such as "terrible," "horrible," or "awful" with emotionally cool words such as "bad," "inconvenient," or "hassle." If the ball goes out of bounds, don't think – "Oh no, this is terrible. I can't win if I hit the ball out of bounds; this will absolutely ruin my game. I know I am going to lose." Instead, use positive self-talk and think – "I don't like this situation, but I handle it as well as anybody, and I can deal with it. I can recover from this. I can cope with this situation and still have a good game."

Analyze your own self-talk in competition. Negative self-talk is a habit developed over time. It likewise takes time (days or even weeks) to learn to replace negative self-talk with the productive habit of positive self-talk. Instead of focusing on the negative (i.e., what you can't do or what is wrong), focus on the positive (i.e., what you can do; what you want to do; what is right). Not only will this focus on success, it will build confidence and positively impact your performance.

Mental Skills: Use Positive Self-Talk to Build Confidence

Successful athletes are confident. Confidence is developed over time through a combination of positive thinking and success experiences. Confident athletes consistently use constructive thinking to focus on and benefit from their successes and to minimize errors and losses. Confidence enables us to trust our performance.

Competition involves setbacks, obstacles, and disappointments; the successful athlete must respond optimistically (i.e., focus on what I *can do*) rather than focusing on the negative (i.e., what is wrong or undesirable) to remain confident and to perform well. Poor performance and errors should be viewed as an exception to your typical good performance; that is, the error reflects only one shot, one play, or one game. Successful performance should be expected and should be thought of as representative of your actual ability. This positive mindset will help build resilience; that is, the ability to overcome challenges, adapt in the face of adversity, and quickly recover from setbacks and difficulties.

Confident athletes think they *can*. They use positive self-talk and positive imagery to focus on positive performance rather than worrying about past or future poor performance or the possible negative outcome of poor execution. The defining trait of a successful athlete is the ability to focus on the positive aspects of his/her game even when faced with challenges and obstacles. This builds confidence, which, in turn, programs the athlete for success on the court/field/course. For example, few athletes enjoy playing in the rain. If it is raining, rather than telling yourself how poorly you play in the rain, think to yourself that you can hit the ball in the rain as well as the next guy/gal.

Athletes can control their thoughts. They can use positive self-talk to build confidence and enhance performance. Successful athletes learn to replace negative self-defeating thoughts with positive, confident ones and with expectations for success. Building confidence requires a conscious effort to stop negative self-talk and negative memories, and to replace these with positive self-talk focusing on what the athlete can do and what is right about the situation. Next time you are in competition, put 15–20 paper clips in your right pocket. Each time you catch yourself engaging in a negative thought (e.g., "What a terrible situation." "I can't hit that." "That shot blew the whole game."), move a paper clip to the left pocket. At the end of the game, the number of clips in the left pocket will let you know how often these destructive thoughts are hindering your game. If you don't have pockets, put a rubber band around your wrist and snap it each time you catch yourself using negative self-talk. Use that little sting to snap you back to the positive. Learn to recognize negative self-talk and replace it with positive self-talk. Positive self-talk can be as simple as "I don't like to perform in this situation, but I have done it before and I can do it now." The key is to (1) recognize negative self-talk, (2) stop negative self-talk, and (3) replace negative self-talk with positive self-talk.

Affirmation statements are short positive phrases that are a ready form of positive self-talk that can boost confidence. Affirmation statements can capture the keys to effective performance such as Mohammed Ali saying "Float like a butterfly, sting like a bee" to enhance his footwork and the force of his blows. This affirmation statement serves as a performance cue to signal the key to effective skill execution. Likewise, consider Ali's general affirmation statement, "I am the greatest!" When you hear positive affirmations often enough, you believe them. You can develop affirmation statements for the key skills in your sport and have them ready when you need them in practice or competition to help ensure you use positive self-talk.

Athletes think about their game. However, it is not simply thinking that disrupts performance; it is negative thinking. Successful athletes learn to control their self-talk and eliminate negative thoughts that disrupt their performance. Doubt and negativity lead to hesitation and an inability to trust your performance. Virtually every coach will tell you that after you have practiced many reps and are ready to perform, you need to stop thinking and trust your skills. Positive self-talk will build the confidence that will enable you to have that trust. Learn to replace negative thoughts with positive self-talk to build confidence and improve your performance.

Mental Skills: Focus on the "3 Ps"

Mental skills can aid your performance as much as physical skills. We probably recognize the importance of focus in improving our game. However, many of us find ourselves distracted even as we attempt to set up for the next play/event. The key to focus in competition or any other situation is self-talk. Self-talk is what we say to ourselves, whether it is aloud or silent thoughts. Each of us has limited attentional space (i.e., the part of our mind that allows us to pay attention). If we allow distractions to enter into this limited attention, we have less attention left for focusing on our current actions. There are three keys to proper attentional focus. They are focus on the Present; focus on the Positive, and focus on the Performance. These are referred to as the "3 Ps" of effective focus.

The first "P" refers to the Present. In a performance situation, such as on the court or field, the power is in the present. The past is history – you cannot change it. The future is a mystery and cannot be impacted at this moment. The one point in time we can impact is right now – the Present. If you are thinking about your past performance (good or poor) or the score or outcome for the game or match, then you are not fully focused on the present play. You are using your limited attentional space to focus on things you cannot impact. After the game is over or the match is completed, you may effectively review your performance. However, while you are competing, your full attention should be on the present play at hand.

The second "P" refers to Positive. We should focus on the correct, positive performance we would like to accomplish. There is a strong mind–body connection such that your body responds to what your mind is thinking. However, the response is largely to the action (or verb) in the self-talk statement; the body does not hear the "do" or "don't." Thus, saying, "keep my eye on the ball" is much more effective than saying, "don't take my eye off the ball." What the body responds to in the latter is "... take my eye off the ball" – the action, not the "don't." Have you ever wondered why you tell yourself "I don't want to hit the ball out of bounds," then hit the ball right out of bounds? Your body is simply responding to what your self-talk is telling it to do, "... hit the ball out of bounds." Thus, it is important to use Positive Self-Talk. Tell yourself "I want to keep the ball on the left side of the court/field" and you will get much better results. After you have taken your swing/shot/pitch, etc., if there is time, you can reinforce good performance by visualizing the successful performance. If the performance was not what you desired, visualize yourself performing correctly; then move on to the next play and give it your full attention.

The final "P" stands for Performance. Focus on the performance rather than the outcome. That is, focus on the actual behavior you need to use to accomplish the desired outcome. You may want to win the game, but the only way that can happen is one point at a time. Focusing on your score (i.e., the outcome) rather than each of the points as you play them uses up attentional space. Your full attention is better utilized focusing on the Present Positive Performance you want to accomplish; that is, focus entirely on the performance you are currently executing. Giving your full attention to your current performance is the most effective means of attaining the desired outcome (i.e., winning the game, match, or meet) – see Figures 2.1 and 2.2.

When you are on the court/field/pool, etc. and want to ensure the most effective focus for improving your execution, remember to focus on the "3 Ps": the Present, Positive, Performance.

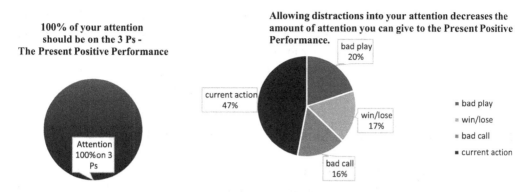

Figure 2.1   The "3 Ps"   **Figure 2.2**   The impact of distractions

Mental Skills: Focus – More than the "3 Ps"

Earlier I indicated the importance of fully focusing on the "3 Ps" (Present, Positive, Performance) in competition. However, there is more to understanding focus. There are two dimensions to focus: direction and breadth.

Direction refers to whether your focus is internally directed to your thoughts or externally directed toward the environment and those in the environment. A fitness swimmer who uses lap time to plan his day and problem solve has an internal focus. Likewise, an alpine skier using imagery to mentally rehearse her race down the slopes has an internal focus. A quarterback dropping back to pass and scanning the field to find an open receiver has an external focus. A basketball player shooting a free throw has an external focus.

The second dimension of focus is breadth. Breadth of focus is on a continuum that ranges from narrow to broad. Think of focus as a zoom lens on a camera that can be narrowed for a close up or widened for a panoramic view. The quarterback searching for a receiver should have a wide focus. The basketball player shooting a free throw should have a narrow focus.

When the two dimensions of focus are combined it results in four different types of focus: broad internal, narrow internal, broad external, and narrow external. The quarterback passing has a broad external focus; the free throw shooter has a narrow external focus. The lap swimmer trying to problem solve has a broad internal focus; the alpine skier using imagery has a narrow internal focus.

Because our focus can be adjusted, we need to learn to control our focus for optimal performance. Essentially, we want to block out irrelevant or distracting information and selectively focus on the information that is critical to our performance. Thus, the quarterback does not want such a broad focus that he is distracted by his girlfriend in the stands; the free throw shooter wants to block out the fans waving their arms behind the goal. For each competitive situation, there likely is an optimal focus. It is up to you and your coach to determine what is best for you in each situation. A volleyball player serving the ball needs a narrow external focus to serve to the target zone. She must then quickly broaden her focus to see where the opponent returns the ball that she may need to pass to her setter. Her focus must be flexible and under her control for optimal performance. If you find yourself distracted by irrelevant aspects of the situation, you likely need to narrow your focus.

If you are missing important cues in the situation, you likely need to broaden focus. If you find yourself too much "in your head," you likely need to focus more externally rather than internally. By learning to control your focus, you will be more effective in adjusting your focus to the aspects of the situation that are critical to effective performance and blocking out distractions.

Key Concepts for Positive Self-Talk, Confidence, and Focus

Positive Self-Talk is intentionally framing what we say to ourselves about a situation in a positive manner, focusing on desired actions and desired outcomes in the situation and what we can do even if it is a challenging situation. Positive self-talk is the opposite of Negative Self-Talk, which frames our thoughts in terms of the negative aspects of a situation and the actions we want to avoid.

Affirmation Statements or Performance Cues are brief statements that capture positive beliefs and actions. When an affirmation statement captures the essence of positive performance, it also is a performance cue.

"3 Ps" – Present, Positive, Performance – are the keys to focus in competition, the positive action you can take right now.

Perspective (The 4th "P") is being able to take a step back and realize what really is important in your life, then putting an error, a missed point, or a lost game/match into perspective. When we have perspective, it is much easier to let go of errors and focus on the positive, which will make us more likely to be successful.

Using Self-Talk to Build Confidence requires having perspective to recognize that errors are atypical and that letting go of errors and focusing on the positive will lead to success.

The Mind–Body Connection means that your body responds to what you are thinking, whether you want it to or not. The body responds to the action/verb in the statement, and ignores the "do" or "don't." This is why it is so important to state things in the positive rather than the negative. Remove the "don't" in the examples below to see what your mind would be telling your body to do and the negative impact that could have on your performance.

- "Don't take your eye off the ball." vs. "Keep your eye on the ball."
- "Don't foul." vs. "Get position. Keep your arms straight up."
- "Don't hit the ball into the net." vs. "Hit the ball down the line."

Note, in Chapter 6 on Relaxation, we will return to the mind–body connection. Not only does the body respond to what the mind is thinking, the mind responds to what the body is doing.

Direction and Breadth of Focus enable us to control our focus much like a zoom lens on a camera. For each situation in competition (and practice) the athlete needs to determine which type of focus (i.e., internal vs. external and narrow vs. broad) is appropriate, to learn to adjust focus to block out distractions and irrelevant information, and to direct focus to those aspects of the situation that will lead to optimal performance.

Chapter 2 Exercises and Techniques

There are several techniques athletes can use to develop positive self-talk. The first of the exercises that follow (Exercise 2.1) involves practicing changing negative self-talk into positive self-talk. Next are exercises that will help you reflect on and correct your own negative self-talk, a Self-Talk Journal, and Reflecting On and Anticipating Negative Self-Talk (Exercises 2.2 to 2.4). Exercise 2.5 will help you with Self-Talk Tracking. It is strongly recommended that you identify up to three focus areas (areas that will benefit from using positive self-talk) and an affirmation statement for each focus area, and that you track your use of positive self-talk for each focus areas. Tracking/measuring is a good technique to ensure that you practice and use positive self-talk. The remaining exercises will help you to focus on techniques beyond self-talk.

Exercise 2.1: Changing Negative Self-Talk to Positive Self-Talk

Below in the left column are examples of negative self-talk. Without looking at the examples of positive self-talk on the right, see if you can come up with positive self-talk to replace the negative examples.

Negative Self-Talk	Positive Self-Talk
I don't want to hit the ball in the water.	*I will hit the ball straight down the fairway.*
I always miss this shot.	*I am good at jump shots.*
I never do well when it is raining.	*We all have to perform in the rain. I can too.*
This shot is impossible. I'll probably shank it.	*This is a tough shot, but I can make it.*
I don't want to miss this serve.	*I am going to nail this serve.*
I hate to play this team. We are going to lose.	*They are a great team, but we can beat them.*
I never play well with this ref.	*Ref makes bad calls, but we can still win.*
This is impossible. I'll probably mess up.	*Good form and technique, and I will score.*

Exercise 2.2: Self-Talk Journal

Start a notebook that you can keep handy to record both positive and negative self-talk. You can make entries before and after practice and before and after competition. Record in the journal the situation in which the self-talk is occurring and what you are saying to yourself. Date each journal entry. For each entry, also record what can be said to replace any negative self-talk with positive self-talk. In particular, especially if the situation is following poor execution, remember to focus on the PRESENT (not the past – it cannot be changed), the POSITIVE (the correct performance you want to accomplish), and PERFORMANCE (repeat to yourself the keys to proper execution). By reflecting and identifying negative self-talk, recording it, and correcting it by writing down what would be positive self-talk in the same situation, you not only create a record of your self-talk, but practice recognizing negative self-talk and changing it to positive self-talk for use in similar situations in the future. If you are using positive self-talk in a challenging situation, job well done!

Complete **Exercise 2.2: Self-Talk Journal**. Read through these examples before you complete the exercise.

Example of a journal entry for a basketball player

1/27 - I was at the free throw line toward the end of the game and was thinking, "If I miss this shot, it could blow the whole game." This was negative self-talk. Instead, I should say, "I am a good free-throw shooter. I can make this shot." And/or "Eyes on the basket and follow through."

Example of a journal entry for a swimmer

10/11 - It was a really tough workout today and I lost motivation about half way into it. I was thinking about what I could get to eat after practice. I remembered that every practice counts. So, I set a goal for the next three sets: First set, I focused on my kick; second set I focused on my stroke; third set I put it all together to have a great swim. Even though I was tired, I had a good practice and coach commented on my effort toward the end of practice.

Example of a journal entry for a golfer

7/8 - It was really hot on the course and the other guys in my foursome were goofing around and not really focusing on practice. I thought, "This weather stinks. I will wait until it cools off to really buckle down and work on my game." I did not do anything productive in practice. When I got home I realized that I wasted the practice time and that if I want to be a good golfer, I have to take it seriously every practice. I reminded myself of the question: What if today makes the difference in getting cut or making the travel team? So, I came up with this affirmation statement to help me stay focused in practice even when it is challenging: "Being my best requires hard work - especially when it is hard to work hard."

Exercise 2.3: Self-Talk Exercise – Reflect and Reconstruct

Use this exercise to review past performance to correct situations where negative self-talk hurt performance and where positive self-talk improved performance.

1. Describe a situation where you were using **negative** self-talk. What was the situation?

What did you "say" (i.e., what you were thinking)?

Because it was negative self-talk, did you stop yourself and refocus on the PRESENT, POSITIVE, PERFORMANCE? If yes, how did you do this? What did you say to yourself?

How did this affect your performance?

2. Describe a situation where you used **positive** self-talk. What was the situation?

What did you "say" (i.e., what you were thinking)?

How did this affect your performance?

Remember this positive self-talk and be prepared to use it when these situations arise in the future.

Complete **Exercise 2.3: Self-Talk Exercise – Reflect and Reconstruct**. Before you complete the exercise, read through these example responses, which are from a basketball player.

Example Reflecting on a Difficult Situation and Changing Negative Self-Talk to Positive Self-Talk and Reflecting on Using Positive Self-Talk

1.   Describe a situation where you were using **negative** self-talk. What was the situation?
We were down by 2 points with only 20 seconds on the clock and I was at the free-throw line.

What did you "say" (i.e., what you were thinking)?
If I miss these shots we are certain to lose the game. I missed my last shot. I don't want to miss this one.

Because it was negative self-talk, did you stop yourself and refocus on the PRESENT, POSITIVE, PERFORMANCE? If yes, how did you do this? What did you say to yourself?
I focused on the "3 Ps". Take one free throw at a time. Use my performance cue BEEF - Balance, Eyes on Target, Elbows In, and Follow Through. Take a deep breath to relax and tell myself, I can make this shot.

How did this affect your performance?
I was more confident. I thought of all of my reps in practice, relaxed and I made the first shot, and then the second shot.

2.   Describe a situation where you used **positive** self-talk. What was the situation?
I was assigned to guard a much taller player.

What did you "say" (i.e., what you were thinking)?
He is a tall guy, but I am quicker and I can defend him if I get position and keep active hands. Coach assigned him to me because he thought I could defend big.

How did this affect your performance?
The positive self-talk made me feel confident that I could defend him and I did a good job on him.

Remember this positive self-talk and be prepared to use it when these situations arise in the future.

Exercise 2.4: Self-Talk – Anticipate Situations

Use this exercise to **anticipate** where you are likely to need to use positive self-talk, then practice so that when the situation comes up in competition, you are comfortable dealing with it.

Identify a competitive situation where you are likely to use negative self-talk (e.g., a frustrating or difficult situation), then write the answer to each question.

Situation: _____

1. What negative thoughts are you likely to have in this situation (i.e., the self-talk that is likely to happen and hurt your performance)?

2. What should you do to focus on the PRESENT?

3. What is the self-talk that will focus on the POSITIVE PERFORMANCE – what are the positive thoughts you should have in this situation? What positive self-talk can you use to replace the negative self-talk?

Remember this positive self-talk and be prepared to use it when this situation arises in the future.

Complete **Exercise 2.4: Self-Talk – Anticipate Situations**. Read through the example answers below before you complete the exercise.

Example of Anticipating a Difficult Situation

Situation

A difficult hole for a golfer: Hole 12, a long par 5 with a water hazard on the right and sand traps by the green.

1. What negative thoughts are you likely to have in this situation (i.e., the self-talk that is likely to happen and hurt your performance)?

I hate this hole - my drive will probably go in the water and my approach shot might end up in the sand. I will be lucky to get a double bogey.

2. What should you do to focus on the PRESENT?

I need to focus on one shot at a time, first on my drive. I will use my performance cue to swing, and think of the target - landing on the left side of the fairway.

3. What is the self-talk that will focus on the POSITIVE PERFORMANCE – what are the positive thoughts you should have in this situation? What positive self-talk can you use to replace the negative self-talk?

I can do this. Let the club do the work. See the target.

Remember this positive self-talk and be prepared to use it when this situation arises in the future.

Exercise 2.5: Self-Talk Tracking and Affirmation Statements for Focus Areas

Identify focus areas. Identify up to three focus areas (you can use exercise sheet 2.5a for this). To identify these, think in terms of specific skills that your coach has told you to target or think of situations where you struggle. These are likely to serve well as focus areas because they are where you are likely to use negative self-talk. Focus areas may be a specific skill (e.g., putting, hitting the ball, etc.), a situation that is challenging for you (e.g., staying focused during play, the 15th hole in golf, after an error, etc.), or more general (e.g., be positive). Focus areas should be tweaked or changed if they are not meeting your needs.

Assess current use of positive self-talk. For each focus area, honestly assess how much of the time you **currently** engage in negative self-talk and positive self-talk (together, these should add up to no more than 100%). You can record these on exercise sheet 2.5a. This will become your baseline to track your progress. Negative self-talk is a habit that develops over time. It likewise will take time to learn to recognize negative self-talk, stop negative self-talk, and replace it with positive self-talk. By recording your progress each week, you will be able to see the improvement you are making, even if it is gradual.

Record percent of positive self-talk each day. Each day that you are practicing or competing (or thinking about your sport) record what percent of your self-talk was positive for each focus area. Record this on exercise sheet 2.5b each day. Look at your baseline level of positive self-talk for each focus area and set a realistic, but challenging goal for your positive self-talk for each focus area. (See Chapter 3 on Motivation for guidelines on setting goals for positive self-talk and other aspects of your performance.) Each week you should strive to improve positive self-talk. With practice, positive self-talk should become more and more natural until it becomes how you automatically respond in challenging situations.

Identify affirmation statements. Identify an affirmation statement for each of your focus areas (see exercise sheet 2.5c). The affirmation statement should be something that encourages positive performance. It may be general (e.g., "I am a great free-throw shooter.") or specific and performance related, that is, a performance cue (e.g., Elbows in, follow-through, I will raise the score by 2."). Affirmation statements are readily available positive self-talk. When you cannot come up with on-the-spot positive self-talk (e.g., in the middle of play), you can use your affirmation statement. You also can tape copies of your affirmation statement to your mirror in your bedroom and on your locker. The more you hear your affirmation statement, the more you will believe it, and the more it will positively influence your performance. Write your affirmation statement for each focus area on exercise sheet 2.5c. You may tweak or change your affirmation statement until it works well for you.

Record your use of affirmation statements. Each day record whether or not you used your affirmation statement to help improve performance in each focus area.

Track your progress. Retain your exercise sheets so that as you improve over time you can check where you were when you first started to work on positive self-talk. It will be rewarding to see how much you have improved.

Before you begin **Exercise 2.5: Self-Talk Tracking and Affirmation Statements for Focus Areas** read through these examples of affirmation statements. They may help you when you complete exercise sheet 2.5c.

Examples of Affirmation Statements

"Execute" – used by a champion senior tennis player who liked the pun that he should execute his serve well and, if he did, he would be executing his opponent.

"See the wall, give your all" – used by a swimmer to remind himself to go in strong into the wall at turns.

"Elbow high and it will fly" – used by a volleyball player to indicate that if she keeps her elbow high while hitting, she will return the ball much faster and harder.

You can use this exercise sheet in conjunction with Exercise 2.5: Self-Talk Tracking and Affirmation Statements for Focus Areas.

Exercise sheet 2.5a

Self-Talk Tracking for _____**(date)**

Identify Focus Areas (Fill in the focus areas you identify)

Focus area 1:

Focus area 2:

Focus area 3:

Assess current use of positive self-talk. For each focus area, honestly assess how much of the time you currently engage in negative self-talk and positive self-talk (together, these should add up to no more than 100%). **Reflect on the past week**. What percentage of your thoughts regarding each focus area was negative self-talk and what percentage of your thoughts were positive self-talk.

FOCUS AREA	% Negative Self-Talk	% Positive Self-Talk	Total % Neg + % Pos = 100%
Focus Area 1			
Focus Area 2			
Focus Area 3			

During the week, which days did you consciously work on recognizing and stopping negative self-talk and replacing it with positive self-talk? **Write "yes" or check each day where you worked on positive self-talk for each of your focus areas. Each day fill in the % of self-talk that was positive.**

FOCUS AREA	Monday	Tuesday	Wednesday	Thursday	Friday	Saturday	For the week, % of Self-Talk that was POSITIVE
Focus Area 1							
Focus Area 2							
Focus Area 3							

You can use this exercise sheet in conjunction with Exercise 2.5: Self-Talk Tracking and Affirmation Statements for Focus Areas.

Exercise sheet 2.5b

Affirmation Statements

For each of your focus areas write your affirmation statement(s)/performance cue(s).

Focus Area 1:

Focus Area 2:

Focus Area 3:

During the week, which days did you use your Affirmation Statement(s) for each of your focus areas? **Write "yes" or check each day where you used your Affirmation Statement for your focus area.**

FOCUS AREA	Monday	Tuesday	Wednesday	Thursday	Friday	Saturday
Focus Area 1						
Focus Area 2						
Focus Area 3						

Read through **Exercise 2.5: Self-Talk Tracking and Affirmation Statements for Focus Areas**. Before you complete exercise sheets 2.5a and 2.5b, look through the example responses below. The first example is from an intercollegiate volleyball player who is a defensive specialist focusing in detail on the skill of digging the ball. The second example is from a baseball player working on several areas of his game.

Self-Talk Tracking for September 2 – 9

Identify Focus Areas (Volleyball Defensive Specialist)

Focus area 1: Footwork

Focus area 2: Platform to the Target

Focus area 3: Solid Contact

Assess current use of positive self-talk. For each focus area, honestly assess how much of the time you currently engage in negative self-talk and positive self-talk (together, these should add up to no more than 100%). **Reflect on the past week.** What percentage of your thoughts regarding each focus area was negative self-talk and what percentage of your thoughts were positive self-talk.

FOCUS AREA	% Negative Self-Talk	% Positive Self-Talk	Total % Neg + % Pos = 100%
Focus Area 1	40%	60%	100%
Focus Area 2	65%	35%	100%
Focus Area 3	60%	40%	100%

During the week, which days did you consciously work on recognizing and stopping negative self-talk and replacing it with positive self-talk? **Write "yes" or check each day where you worked on positive self-talk for each of your focus areas. Each day fill in the % of self-talk that was positive.**

FOCUS AREA	Monday	Tuesday	Wednesday	Thursday	Friday	Saturday	For the week, % of Self-Talk that was POSITIVE
Focus Area 1	✓		✓		✓		65%
Focus Area 2	✓	✓		✓	✓		40%
Focus Area 3	✓		✓		✓		55%

Affirmation Statements

For each of your focus areas write your affirmation statement(s)/performance cue(s).

Focus Area 1: FEET THROUGH THE BALL

Focus Area 2: OUT EARLY

Focus Area 3: WATCH IT IN – KEEP STILL

During the week, which days did you use your Affirmation Statement(s) for each of your focus areas? **Write "yes" or check each day where you used your Affirmation Statement for your focus area.**

FOCUS AREA	Monday	Tuesday	Wednesday	Thursday	Friday	Saturday
Focus Area 1	✓		✓		✓	
Focus Area 2	✓	✓		✓	✓	
Focus Area 3	✓		✓		✓	

Self-Talk Tracking for April 1 – 8

Identify Focus Areas (Baseball Player)

Focus area 1: Hitting/Offense

Focus area 2: Fielding/Defense

Focus area 3: Being a Team Leader

Assess current use of positive self-talk. For each focus area, honestly assess how much of the time you currently engage in negative self-talk and positive self-talk (together, these should add up to no more than 100%). **Reflect on the past week.** What percentage of your thoughts regarding each focus area was negative self-talk and what percentage of your thoughts were positive self-talk.

FOCUS AREA	% Negative Self-Talk	% Positive Self-Talk	Total % Neg + % Pos = 100%
Focus Area 1	75%	25%	100%
Focus Area 2	50%	50%	100%
Focus Area 3	60%	40%	100%

During the week, which days did you consciously work on recognizing and stopping negative self-talk and replacing it with positive self-talk? **Write "yes" or check each day where you worked on positive self-talk for each of your focus areas. Each day fill in the % of self-talk that was positive.**

FOCUS AREA	Monday	Tuesday	Wednesday	Thursday	Friday	Saturday	For the week, % of Self-Talk that was POSITIVE
Focus Area 1	✓	✓		✓	✓	✓	35%
Focus Area 2	✓		✓	✓		✓	65%
Focus Area 3	✓	✓		✓	✓	✓	60%

Affirmation Statements

For each of your focus areas write your affirmation statement(s)/performance cue(s).

Focus Area 1: PATIENCE!

Focus Area 2: BRICK WALL – NOTHING GETS THROUGH ME

Focus Area 3: LEAD AND BELIEVE

During the week, which days did you use your Affirmation Statement(s) for each of your focus areas? **Write "yes" or check each day where you used your Affirmation Statement for your focus area.**

FOCUS AREA	Monday	Tuesday	Wednesday	Thursday	Friday	Saturday
Focus Area 1	✓	✓		✓	✓	✓
Focus Area 2	✓	✓	✓	✓		✓
Focus Area 3	✓	✓		✓	✓	✓

Exercise 2.6: Post Your Focus Areas and Affirmation Statements

Affirmation statements and performance cues are positive self-talk statements that are prepared ahead of time to have on the ready when needed in competition. These statements work best when they are so familiar you do not even have to think about them, they automatically enter your thoughts when you are in a performance situation. To ensure your affirmation statements and performance cues are readily available to you in competition, you need to (1) be very familiar with them and (2) use them in practice. One easy technique to help you remember your affirmation statements is to post them in a number of places: in your locker, on your mirror, in the front of your notebook, on the refrigerator –anywhere you look on a regular basis.

For example, at the USA Olympic Swim Trials, Ryan Lochte had "I swim fast" on the front of his t-shirt.

An easier method for making affirmation signs is to create a PowerPoint slide of your focus areas and corresponding affirmation statements, copy the slide, then print the two (identical) slides using the option of two slides to a page. This will result in two framed cards you can cut out and tape to any/all of the places mentioned earlier.

Before you complete **Exercise 2.6: Post Your Focus Areas and Affirmation Statements,** first read through these examples.

Example for a major league baseball pitcher:

FOCUS AREAS	AFFIRMATION STATEMENTS
Stay focused	→ Be aggressive. Be down in the zone.
Slider	→ Get out front. Let it work.
Change up	→ Let the grip do the work. Just throw it.
Focus when complacent	→ Every pitch counts.

Example for an intercollegiate swimmer

FOCUS AREAS	AFFIRMATION STATEMENTS
Turns	→ Head and hips for faster flips.
Underwaters	→ Kick strong. Hold it long.
Be positive	→ Be positive

Example for an intercollegiate athlete trying to focus on school and sports and avoid partying

FOCUS AREAS	AFFIRMATION STATEMENTS
Staying focused	→ No greater thrill than achieving my goal.
Motivation to study	→ Keep your eye on the prize.
Rebounding	→ I bounce back.

Exercise 2.7: Identify Types of Appropriate and Inappropriate Focus

To test your understanding of the direction and breadth of focus, identify the type of focus described in each situation before looking at the answers on page 34. Note that **not all of the examples** are of the appropriate type of focus for the situation described. If the focus is not appropriate, identify the correct type of focus for that situation.

1. A swimmer visualizes her swim while waiting in the natatorium for her event.

2. As a baseball pitcher is winding up to throw a pitch, he notices his girlfriend in the stands.

3. A golfer preparing to tee off thinks to himself that he is three shots back and that he really cannot afford another bogey on this hole.

4. A basketball point guard bringing the ball down the court notes that the other team is in a 2–3 zone defense.

5. A coach reflects on her team's performance during the last competition and plans specific drills for practice to build skills to avoid the same poor performance in future competitions.

6. An athlete takes deep cleansing breaths to relax and clear his head before competing.

Complete **Exercise 2.7: Identify Types of Appropriate and Inappropriate Focus** first, then read through these answers.

Answers to Exercise 2.7

1. narrow internal; appropriate

2. broad external; inappropriate ➔ too broad, needs to narrow his external focus. Note that the pitcher will need a broader focus if there are runners on base than if the bases are empty.

3. narrow internal; inappropriate ➔ needs narrow external focus on this shot, focusing on the "3 Ps". Note the negative self-talk of focusing on what he wants to avoid rather than on what he hopes to accomplish.

4. broad external; appropriate

5. broad internal; appropriate

6. narrow internal; appropriate

Exercise 2.8: Focus Technique – Putting Distractions on Hold

Key Points for Athletes

1. During competition (and practice) you need to be fully focused on your performance.
   a. You cannot:
      i. Study for an upcoming exam (or do other homework)
      ii. Talk to your family, friends, or significant other
      iii. Take a nap
      iv. Run errands
      v. Other distractions
   b. All of these distractions will still be there when the competition or practice is over.

2. The human mind works to remind us of important things we need to do – unless we have some sort of closure.
   a. If the distractions are still active, your mind will tend to wander to those distractions unless you take some action to stop it.
      i. You can either gain closure on the distraction – or –
      ii. You can ensure your mind that you will remember to deal with it later.
   b. This technique, described on page 36, accomplishes the latter – that is, it ensures you will remember your distractions/to-do-list later.

These notes, for the coach, describe a practical technique for putting distractions on hold. They can be used in conjunction with **Exercise 2.8: Focus Technique – Putting Distractions on Hold**.

1. Coach – get enough small (5 × 7 – but any size will work) manila envelopes for each player to have his/her own envelope.
2. Give each player an envelope and have him/her write his/her name on the envelope.
3. Before each competition (or practice), have each player write down on a sheet of paper anything s/he needs to remember that could serve as a distraction during the competition (or practice).
4. Each player should put his/her list of distractions in the envelope and turn the envelope into the coach (or put the envelope in their locker).
5. The coach will **not** look in the envelopes, but will put them away until after the competition (or practice).
6. During competition (or practice) the athlete can be fully focused on performing well and can rest assured that the items on the list will still be available for their attention after the competition (or practice) is over.
7. After the competition (or practice), the coach should return each envelope to the appropriate player.
8. The player should take his/her list out of the envelope and return the envelope to the coach – so, the envelopes can be used for the next competition or practice.
9. The player now has his/her to-do list.

Most teams already do something like this with cell phones to prevent the players from being distracted by their phone. However, it is much harder to turn off the mind. Taking this step to let your mind know that your distraction list will ensure that you will remember helps to prevent the mind wandering to the distraction during the match (or practice).

Of course, individual athletes may use this technique for themselves even if the entire team does not participate.

Exercise 2.9: Focusing Through Distractions

These two exercises will help you learn to control your focus and to block out distractions.

Exercise 2.9a: 30-Second Focus

1. You will learn to focus for 30 seconds.
    *   Set a timer for 30 seconds.
    *   Chose something in your environment to focus on for the full 30 seconds.
    *   Start the timer and start your focusing.

What you choose to focus on can be simple, such as a piece of equipment used in your sport, a painting on the wall, your friend's face, or close your eyes and listen to the ambient noises in the room, etc.

2. Try to recall whether you were able to focus for the full 30 seconds or were you distracted by some other thoughts, sounds, smells, or sights.
3. Repeat this exercise until you can remain fully focused on any subject you chose for the full 30 seconds.

Exercise 2.9b: Changing Channels

1. Turn on two different radio stations (you may use TV or one of each – but if you use TV, ensure it is a talking show (e.g., news, weather, etc.) rather than mostly visual).
2. Set a timer for 1 minute, then 2 minutes, then 3 minutes, up to 5 minutes as you get better at focusing and blocking out distractions.
3. Choose one of the broadcasts to block out and the other to listen to and really focus on for the full time (1, 2, 3, 4, or 5 minutes) such that you can repeat what was said in the broadcast when the timer goes off.
4. Once you have mastered this, set multiple timers to go off at 2-minute intervals. When the timer goes off, switch your focus to the other story while blocking out the first. Each time the timer rings, refocus on the other story and block out the one you were listening to. Repeat this sequence of switching back and forth until you can easily focus and block out which ever signal you target.

Motivation   **3**

Athletes, coaches, and business leaders all recognize the importance of motivation in achieving performance excellence. Motivation is what initiates, directs, and maintains our efforts toward an outcome. Psychologists refer to motivation as a "psychological construct." As with leadership, personality, and other constructs, we cannot see motivation nor can we measure it directly. But we know motivation and these other constructs exist because of their manifestation in behavior. A simple but useful formula for predicting the level of performance is Performance = Ability × Motivation. That is, motivation and ability are compensatory factors in determining performance. We know an athlete with enormous ability will fail if s/he is not motivated. Likewise, we all know an athlete with lesser ability who outperforms those with more ability because s/he is highly motivated. Accordingly, regardless of one's ability level, a high level of motivation will result in better performance.

Theories of Motivation

There are many theories of motivation. Three very useful theories are Reinforcement Theory, Instrumentality Theory, and Goal Setting Theory. I will briefly address the first two and go into detail with the third.

Reinforcement Theory

We are motivated by the consequences of our behavior. We tend to repeat behavior that leads to satisfying outcomes and eliminate behavior that results in negative outcomes. Satisfying outcomes are referred to as reinforcement. Positive reinforcement means we obtain something desirable following the behavior (e.g., a trophy, a hug, ice cream, money). Negative reinforcement means something undesirable is removed following the behavior (e.g., nagging stops, the alarm clock stops ringing, 6 a.m. workouts stop). A behavior followed by either positive or negative reinforcement *makes it more likely we will repeat the behavior in the future* in similar situations. In fact, when we repeat a behavior that seems illogical, it is likely something reinforcing follows that behavior. For example, an extrovert who likes attention may irritate the coach because the attention from the coach (and perhaps teammates) is reinforcing and outweighs the scolding from the coach.

This brings us to another component of Reinforcement Theory: punishment. Punishment is an undesirable consequence following a behavior that *decreases the likelihood the behavior will occur again in the future* (e.g., extra workouts, scolding, removal of privileges). Generally, reinforcement is preferred over punishment in shaping behavior. Punishment can go awry in several ways, such as rather than stopping the undesired behavior the individual (a) learns to avoid the person who punishes, (b) learns to refrain from the negative behavior when the punisher is present, and/or (c) becomes angry because of the punishment. From a mental skills perspective, perhaps the biggest problem with punishment is that it only identifies the negative behavior to be avoided and provides no direction for the desired, positive performance. Positive reinforcement indicates the desired, positive performance. Punishment should be used only to deter a specific and particularly disruptive, maladaptive, or damaging behavior.

To apply reinforcement theory, think in terms of the outcomes of your actions. Can you create positive outcome contingencies for a desired behavior that you currently fail to perform? For example, you can reward yourself for completing a challenging workout, losing weight, gaining muscle, or taking the first step to resolve a conflict with a teammate. Identify a component of your sport for which you would like to increase motivation. Then identify a reasonable reward you can provide yourself if you successfully complete the challenging activity.

Instrumentality Theory

Instrumentality theory is also called Valence, Instrumentality, and Expectancy Theory or VIE Theory. Similar to Reinforcement Theory, VIE Theory involves outcomes, but VIE focuses on the cognitive/thinking processes involved. Essentially, VIE Theory indicates that we will work harder for outcomes that we value. Expectancy refers to the expectations we have that if we attempt a given behavior we can execute that behavior; thus, Expectancy is similar to the construct of self-efficacy. Instrumentality refers to the actual process of obtaining an outcome by engaging in a given performance. For example, if we engage in exercise regularly and eat healthily, we will maintain a desirable weight. Valence refers to the value we place on an outcome. For any complex behavior, there will be both positive and negative outcomes. When, for a given behavior, the positive outcomes outweigh the negative outcomes, we will pursue that behavior. For example, most people would rather sleep in than get up early to work out. However, if early workouts mean that we will develop the strength, stamina, and skill that will help us be successful in competition – outcomes with high valence for many athletes – we will choose the early workouts over sleeping in. VIE is important in explaining why athletes work so hard to be successful in their sport. Athletes expect their behavior will lead to the outcomes they value; thus, it is worth the effort.

Intrinsic versus Extrinsic Motivation

The value we place on an outcome may be internally/intrinsically driven or externally/extrinsically driven. Intrinsically motivated behavior is behavior we engage in because it is inherently rewarding. Characteristics of the task combine with our personal values to result in a rewarding positive feeling, enjoyment, or a sense of wellbeing when we successfully complete the task. For many athletes, performing well in their sport is intrinsically motivating.

Extrinsically motivated behavior is behavior we engage in because of external rewards such as money; trophies; or pleasing others such as parents, coaches, or significant others. There is nothing inherently wrong with extrinsic motivation. However, intrinsic motivation tends to be more long lasting and to promote more dedication and persistence in working toward task accomplishment than does extrinsic motivation. Typically, if extrinsic motivation is removed, effort ceases.

Importantly, most behavior is multiply determined. That is, most of the time, there are a number of forces motiving our behavior. These forces may be intrinsic and/or extrinsic. For example, athletes who work hard to excel at their sport likely are intrinsically motivated, yet they also enjoy trophies, the coach's praise, and admiration from peers.

Mental Skills: Goal Setting

One mark of a mentally tough athlete is the ability to focus attention and effort on key components of his/her performance. Goal setting is a relatively simple, straightforward motivational technique that can focus your efforts and improve your performance. However, there are several important characteristics that must be present for goals to be effective.

First, goals must be accepted and understood. Goals that are thrust upon us, that we neither understand nor believe in, will not help our performance. If a coach assigns a goal to you and you are not exactly sure what the goal is or how to accomplish it, ask for clarification.

Second, goals should be specific and should be challenging. Specific goals have been proven to be much more effective than vague "Do your best" goals. Rather than using the general goal of "Play a good game," set a more specific goal such as "Improve my hitting percentage by 10%." Challenging goals that are difficult but realistic (i.e., the goal is attainable) will improve our performance much more effectively than will easy goals. We tend to dismiss unrealistic goals – so they fail our first criterion.

Third, goals should be measurable. What is a measurable goal? Ask yourself "How will I know if I have accomplished this goal?" If you can provide an answer to that question, your goal likely is measurable. If possible, quantify your goal. However, quantifying goals is not always possible or necessary.

Fourth, keep track of your performance in relation to your goal. At the end of the match/game determine if you met your goal. This feedback is a source of motivation and may provide information to improve your strategy for attaining your goal. If you attained your goal, pat yourself on the back! Now set a goal for the next time you play. Is there room for further improvement or do you want to strive to maintain your current good performance? If you failed to meet your goal, can you determine why it was not attained? Was it strategy, effort, lack of focus, or perhaps some extenuating circumstance? The answer(s) to this question provide you with information to modify your play the next time you perform. **Feedback in relation to your goal is essential for goal setting to be effective.**

Finally, goals may be set for outcomes or for the process (performance) that is necessary to reach an outcome. Long-range goals are frequently stated in terms of outcomes. However, the shorter the timeframe for the goal, the more important it is that the goal focuses on the process. For example, your goal may be to get a bid to the NCAA Tournament. This is an outcome goal. However, when you are preparing for a specific match/game, your goal setting will be more effective if you state your goal for that game in terms of process – for example, "My goal for this game is to focus on defense by ensuring that I am in position every play." This goal is focusing on the process you will use immediately to help you attain your more long-range goal of winning the game and eventually getting the bid to the NCAA Tournament.

You may use the acronym "SMART" to remember the characteristics of effective goals: "S" for Specific, "M" for Measurable, "A" for Achievement Oriented, "R" for Realistic, and "T" for Timely. Use "SMART" goals to focus on the dimensions of your game you would like to improve. If you are working on offense, set a goal for hitting (e.g., target a challenging hitting percentage). After each game, see how well you did, then set a goal for the next game. Do you need to change your strategy? Increase your goal? If you are focusing on defense, set a goal and keep track of whether or not you achieve the goal each game or each day in practice.

Goal setting can be used by virtually anybody to improve performance in competition, at work, or in your personal life. Follow these guidelines and see how effective goal setting can be for you.

Goal Orientation. To conclude, I will mention the construct of goal orientation. Goal orientation refers to how one views their ability in relation to success in a performance context. Those with a *growth/learning orientation* view ability as malleable, seek to master new skills, and see failure to reach a goal as an indication that more effort, training, or better strategy is needed. Those with a *performance orientation* view ability as fixed, seek to demonstrate their current level of ability, and see failure to reach a goal as an indication that they do not have what it takes to be successful. Those with a growth orientation seek feedback, persist in the face of difficulty, set higher subsequent goals, and are more likely to achieve higher levels of performance. Those with a performance orientation are more likely to focus on avoiding failure, are likely give up when the going gets tough and/or to set lower subsequent goals.

Goal orientation is considered to be situation specific (i.e., you may have different orientations in different situations) and somewhat malleable (i.e., we can change our orientation for a given situation). Generally, a growth/learning orientation is more productive and leads to more success than does a performance orientation. Thus, when you fail to accomplish your goal, try to respond with a growth orientation to help ensure future success.

Key Concepts for Motivation

Goal setting is an important motivational technique. You should set SMART goals for key outcomes and the processes needed to achieve these outcomes. The key performance components in your sport likely define the processes needed to reach desired outcomes. Goals will focus your efforts, and feedback in relation to these goals will provide cues for continuously improving your performance. Establish rewards for accomplishing your goals for important components of your sport. The rewards need only be something that is meaningful to you and should be proportional to the effort it took to stay focused and accomplish your goal.

Set difficult but realistic goals. In bowling, a score of 300 represents a perfect game and likely only the best bowlers can realistically throw a perfect game. In several sports (e.g., 3-point goals in basketball, hitting in volleyball, hitting in baseball and softball), 30%/300/.300 is considered to be a threshold for excellent performance. When setting goals, consider your current level of performance and where you would like your performance to be. I have worked with All American volleyball players who averaged greater than .400 hitting for a season. I have also worked with other good intercollegiate players who average just over .200 for the season. It may be that you need to set a series of goals over time reflecting incremental performance toward your long-term goal. If you currently are hitting .280, then .300 may be realistic for you. I had a baseball player ask me how to stay confident when you know that seven times out of ten you will not get a hit. The answer is perspective and positive self-talk. You must use positive self-talk to expect to get a hit every time you take a shot or swing or step to the plate. However, after a miss, you must keep your perspective and know that when you get a hit/kill three times out of ten, you are performing well. Put the misses behind you, and focus on the "3 Ps" – the Present, Positive, Performance.

Behavior is Multiply Determined. There rarely is a simple way to motivate an athlete over the long, demanding practices required for performance excellence. Typically, a combination of intrinsic and extrinsic motivation can work together to help maintain motivation. For example, I worked with an Olympic swimmer who practiced six hours a day, six days a week. She used a number of motivational techniques to maintain her focus and her effort. Likely the most important source of motivation was her intrinsic desire to be an Olympic swimmer. She set goals and tracked her performance for key components of her swim (e.g., turns, underwaters) and for using her mental skills (e.g., positive self-talk, imagery). She also used some simple techniques such as pennies on the side of the pool, sliding one over each time she completed a set in a long, difficult practice so that she could visually see her progress toward completing the practice session. Finally, she felt gratitude to her family for supporting her while she trained to achieve her dream and who were there to witness her win gold in the 2012 Olympics.

Determine what you value and work hard to accomplish it. Recognize that to achieve excellence in your sport likely means you will have to give up some activities you might otherwise enjoy (e.g., indulgent eating habits, sleeping late in the mornings, spending more time with non-sport friends, etc.), and that you likely will have to engage in some activities that are difficult and challenging (e.g., demanding practices, strict workout schedules, getting enough sleep, eating healthy, etc.). If performance excellence was easy, everyone would do it; but it is not. If performance excellence is of great value to you, when you achieve your performance goals, you will be very satisfied and recognize that the effort was well worthwhile.

Chapter 3 Exercises and Techniques

The exercises for Chapter 3 target effective goal setting. Exercise 3.1 provides a worksheet (3.1a) to help ensure your goals contain the important elements for goal success. Two examples of completed goal setting worksheets follow. Exercise 3.2 is a checklist to help ensure you set effective goals. Exercise 3.3 illustrates several different methods for tracking performance in relation to goals. Finally, Exercise 3.4 presents the Goal Setting-Satisfaction Paradox and is designed for those athletes who are overly harsh critics of their own performance and may have perfectionist tendencies.

Exercise 3.1: Setting goals

The goal setting sheet that follows (exercise sheet 3.1a) will help you work through the goals that are important to your success in your sport. You will need to identify the important outcomes you would like to accomplish and the key processes/skills you will need to develop to reach those goals. You might think about the focus areas you identified for positive self-talk, key areas your coach has indicated you need to work on, or key skills that you would like to improve. If you participate in a team sport, think in terms of your roles and responsibilities on the team.

First, you need to identify the important outcome you would like to work on. Note that goals can be set for multiple outcomes and processes. In general, it is advised you keep your overarching goals limited to about three with two or three process goals/intermediate goals for each overarching goal. If you are new to goal setting, you might wish to focus on only one outcome goal. As you gain experience with goal setting, you can add additional goals. You can refer to the goal setting checklist in Exercise 3.2 to ensure you have written sound goal statements.

You can use this exercise sheet in conjunction with **Exercise 3.1: Setting Goals**.

Exercise sheet 3.1a

Identify a challenging goal that is important to you that you would like to accomplish within the next 12 months. Below, clearly state the goal in specific terms. Ensure your goal is a SMART goal (i.e., Specific, Measurable, Achievement Oriented, Realistic, Timely).

GOAL:

The above goal likely should have been an *outcome* goal and a *long-term* goal. What are some *process goals* or *short-term/proximal* goals that will facilitate accomplishing your goal?

PROCESS GOAL 1:

PROCESS GOAL 2:

Do you know how to accomplish your long-term goal and do you have the knowledge, skills, and abilities to accomplish your goal? If the answer to either is "No," you may need to include *learning goals* as well. Below list any learning goals that will facilitate accomplishing your long-term goal.

LEARNING GOAL 1:

LEARNING GOAL 2:

How will you track your performance in relation to your goal? What type of feedback will you have to inform you of whether or not you are on track to accomplish your goal and whether or not you need to modify your strategy to accomplish your goal? How will you know that you have accomplished your goal?

FEEDBACK 1:

FEEDBACK 2:

FEEDBACK 3:

Read through **Exercise 3.1: Setting Goals**. Before you complete exercise sheet 3.1a, look through the example responses that follow.

Setting Goals Example 1: Basketball

GOAL: To improve free throw shooting average to above 70%
The above goal likely should have been an *outcome* goal and a *long-term* goal. What are some *process goals* or *short-term/proximal* goals that will facilitate accomplishing your goal?

PROCESS GOAL 1: To develop a routine for shooting free-throws and use it every time I shoot a free-throw in practice and in games

PROCESS GOAL 2: To use imagery to practice my free throws outside of practice (e.g., traveling on the bus, in the evening when relaxing before going to sleep)

Do you know how to accomplish your long-term goal and do you have the knowledge, skills, and abilities to accomplish your goal? If the answer to either is "No," you may need to include *learning goals* as well. Below, list any learning goals that will facilitate accomplishing your long-term goal.

LEARNING GOAL 1: I need to check with coach for the keys to good shooting mechanics/technique for free throws.

LEARNING GOAL 2: I need to learn how to use imagery. I will work with my sport psychologist to learn imagery and visualization (or read Chapter 4).

How will you track your performance in relation to your goal? What type of feedback will you have to inform you of whether or not you are on track to accomplish your goal and whether or not you need to modify your strategy to accomplish your goal? How will you know that you have accomplished your goal?

FEEDBACK 1: I will chart my free throw percentage in practice every day and check the stats after each game. If my percentage is off, I will check with coach on my technique.

FEEDBACK 2: I will record what percentage of my free throws I used my routine.

FEEDBACK 3: I will track how many days a week I used imagery to practice free throws.

Setting Goals Example 2: Volleyball

GOAL: To get at least 50 blocks this season

The above goal likely should have been an *outcome* goal and a *long-term* goal. What are some *process goals* or *short-term/proximal* goals that will facilitate accomplishing your goal?

PROCESS GOAL 1: To consistently focus on blocking mechanics and technique in practice

PROCESS GOAL 2: To use positive self-talk to help automate good technique. Use affirmation statement/performance cue of "Hands set, press over the net."

Do you know how to accomplish your long-term goal and do you have the knowledge, skills, and abilities to accomplish your goal? If the answer to either is "No," you may need to include *learning goals* as well. Below list any learning goals that will facilitate accomplishing your long-term goal.

LEARNING GOAL 1: Work with coach to ensure good mechanics

LEARNING GOAL 2:

How will you track your performance in relation to your goal? What type of feedback will you have to inform you of whether or not you are on track to accomplish your goal and whether or not you need to modify your strategy to accomplish your goal? How will you know that you have accomplished your goal?

FEEDBACK 1: After each practice, I will reflect and self-evaluate and chart what percentage of the time I used good technique when blocking.

FEEDBACK 2: I will record the number of blocks in each match and keep a running total over the season. I need to average 1.4 blocks per match.

FEEDBACK 3: I will ask coach for feedback on my blocking when I do not block well in a match.

Exercise 3.2: A Checklist to Ensure Effective Goals

Use the checklist below to ensure your goals have the proper characteristics to work effectively.

1. Are your goal statements specific? Is what you hope to accomplish clearly stated?
2. Are your goals challenging/difficult, but realistic?
3. Are your goals related to important aspects of your performance?
4. Are your goals consistent with your individual and team priorities and objectives?
5. Do you have measurable quantitative or qualitative indicators of goal performance?
6. Do you have a realistic time frame for achieving each goal?
7. Do you have the knowledge, skill, and ability (KSAs) to accomplish these goals? If not, what KSAs do you need to develop and how will you develop them?

_____

_____

8. What are the resources needed to accomplish these goals?

_____

_____

Do you have the resources to accomplish these goals? If not, how will you acquire the resources?

_____

_____

9. a. Are your process goals comprehensive?

   b. Or do you need additional action plans to provide a clear path to goal accomplishment?

Exercise 3.3: Examples of Techniques to Track Performance Relative to Goals to Provide Feedback

For goals to be effective, they must be paired with feedback. That is, feedback is essential to successfully using goals to improve your performance. Think about feedback you may have received in the past and how it helped you improve your performance.

Feedback serves two primary purposes. First, most individuals find feedback inherently rewarding. Think about when you take a test; even if you think you may not have performed as well as you would have liked, you likely wanted to know how you did on the test. Second, feedback performs a cueing function. That is, feedback can tell you how you need to modify your behavior to be successful in the future. You may need to put forth more effort, to focus your efforts on a different component of your sport, or to change strategy. Feedback also lets you know if what you currently are doing is successful so that there is no need to change, just maintain your current behavior.

There are many techniques for obtaining feedback about your performance. In competition, feedback is almost always present in terms of the score and a variety of statistics kept for the sport. Coaches provide feedback during practice and in competition. You likely will find it useful to track your own performance in your focus areas identified for positive self-talk and for goal setting. Here are some simple examples that illustrate a few of the many ways you can track your performance in relation to your goals. Think about which ones may work for you.

Example 1

This chart was used by an Olympic swimmer to help her focus on speed in each half of her 100m race by using the affirmation statements/performance cues of "Attack Strong" and "Pain to Attain" respectively for the first and second 50 meters of her swim. Her goal was to use these affirmation statements at least 80% of the time during practice. She charted each day this focus was a part of practice.

Percent of Time	Accelerate First 50	Finish Fast Second 50
100		
90	*	
80	Goal = 80% *	
70		
60		
50		
40		

For this particular practice, the "★" on the chart indicates that she used the performance cue "Attack Strong" and accelerated the first 50 meters approximately 90% of the time, and used the performance cue "Pain to Attain" and finished strong approximately 80% of the time.

Example 2

The focus areas and blank chart that follow were used by the same Olympic swimmer to work on imagery for her event, the 100m fly. Two weeks before a big meet, she would use imagery daily to ensure key components of her swim were correct. Notice focus area 5 is the complete swim where she would visualize swimming her event from start to finish. Other focus areas were to help her fine tune specific skill components. Simply checking off when she used her visualization was sufficient motivation and feedback to focus her time and efforts on her visualization.

Focus area 1: KICKING
Focus area 2: ACCELERATE
Focus area 3: HEAD DOWN
Focus area 4: BODY POSITION
Focus area 5: WHOLE EVENT

During the week, which days did you consciously work on visualizing each of the five focus areas? Each day fill in "Yes" or "No" to indicate when you used visualization for each focus area.

FOCUS AREA	Monday	Tuesday	Wednesday	Thursday	Friday	Saturday	Sunday
Focus area 1							
Focus area 2							
Focus area 3							
Focus area 4							
Focus area 5							

Example 3

The same Olympic swimmer used the blank chart that follows to track how often she maintained good form throughout her swim in practice. As the Olympic trials drew near, her goal was to maintain good form 100% of the time. However, when we first started working together nine months before the trials, her goal was to maintain good from at least 60% of the time. As her swimming improved, she gradually raised her goal. By tracking her performance each week (and dating and saving her charts), the feedback provided in relation to her goal enabled the swimmer to track progress over time. The progress was gradual, but by tracking progress in relation to each weekly goal, the great progress made over the months of practice could be seen.

100 FLY – MAINTAIN STROKE GOAL
Estimate % of Times You Maintained your Stroke

WEEK:						
%	Monday	Tuesday	Wednesday	Thursday	Friday	Saturday
100	GOAL – 100%					
90						
80						
70						
60						
50						
40						
30						
20						
10						
0						

Exercise 3.4: The Goal Setting–Satisfaction Paradox

It is not uncommon for athletes who are extremely competitive and achievement oriented to have unrealistically high expectations for themselves. Those with perfectionistic tendencies frequently are overly harsh critics of their own performance. Perfectionistic tendencies can lead to feelings of disappointment even after good performance. Statistics are kept for various performance components/skills in every sport. Examples include shooting percentage, batting average, ace to error ratio, average putts per green, etc. Each statistic reflects a ratio of success to errors. It is a fact that errors are made by even the most successful athletes. Thus, on one level, athletes know they cannot be perfect, yet some athletes still maintain a goal of (near) perfection. This exercise helps athletes understand how to set realistic goals and how setting unrealistically high goals can lead to feelings of disappointment and dissatisfaction. Follow the steps on exercise worksheet 3.4a to complete this task for yourself.

You can use this exercise sheet in conjunction with **Exercise 3.4: The Goal Setting–Satisfaction Paradox**.

Exercise sheet 3.4a

1. First, recognize that no athlete (including you) can be perfect.
2. Below is a scale that ranges from very poor performance to average performance to good performance to perfect performance (Figure 3.1).

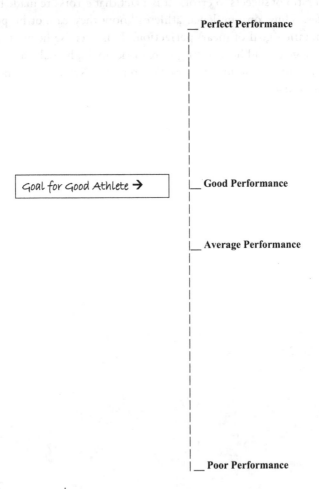

Figure 3.1 Performance scale

Note the mark on the scale for an athlete at your level of competition who is good at your sport and who has set his/her performance goal at Good – s/he is targeting performing at a better than Average, Good level. We will refer to this person as the Good Athlete.

3. Mark on Figure 3.1 where you think your performance goal should be.
   Chances are you marked your goal well above Good and a bit below Perfect (as shown in Figure 3.2).
4. Now, let's say both you and the Good Athlete have performed and your actual performance levels are indicated by the vertical arrows below in Figure 3.2.

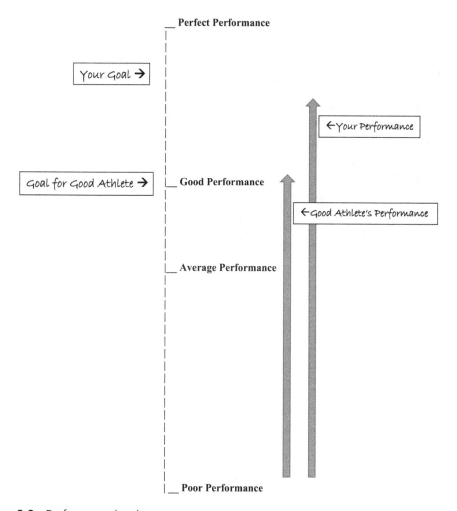

Figure 3.2 Performance levels

Let's examine the reactions of the Good Athlete. S/he achieved his/her performance goal and feels good about it. S/he is satisfied with his/her performance.

Now let's examine your reaction. Your performance exceeded that of the Good Athlete, but did not reach your extremely high (and likely unrealistic) goal. You likely feel bad and are dissatisfied with your performance because you failed to reach your goal. You have these negative feelings even though your performance surpassed the Good mark and significantly exceeded the performance of the Good Athlete (who is satisfied with his/her performance).

This is the Goal Setting–Satisfaction Paradox. Even though you out-performed the Good Athlete, you are dissatisfied with your performance. Realistically, you should be pleased with your high, successful performance. Because of perfectionistic tendencies and setting unrealistically high goals, you miss the opportunity to be pleased with your performance and to enjoy the satisfaction of a job well done.

After completing exercise sheet 3.4a, read the lessons learned below.

Lessons Learned

1. **DO NOT** lower your goals to avoid the paradox. Your high goals pull your performance to a higher level than it would be if you set lower goals. If you had set your goal at Good, you likely would have achieved the Good level of performance rather than exceeding the Good level. Setting high/challenging realistic goals will improve your performance.
2. **DO** recognize how tough your goals are and, when you perform well, feel good about it. Pat yourself on the back and enjoy your success even if you did not reach your extremely high (unrealistic) goal. This perspective will increase your satisfaction with your performance and help you maintain motivation to continue to work hard at your sport.

Imagery

4

Imagery, visualization, and mental rehearsal are all terms that refer to seeing with the mind's eye – that is, the ability to form a controlled mental image that can be manipulated to improve performance. Mental rehearsal is using imagery or visualization to practice a skill or performance using only your mind. Interestingly, scientific studies have shown that when those who are skilled in imagery mentally rehearse a performance, the electrical signals between muscles and neurons are the same as when that performance is actually physically executed. Thus, mental rehearsal can provide repetitions to build muscle memory just like physical practice. Unfortunately for the lazy ones, mental rehearsal is best used as a supplement to physical practice, not as a substitute. When combined with physical practice, mental rehearsal leads to better performance than physical practice alone.

Mental Skills: Imagery for Performance Enhancement

Whether we recognize it or not, most of us use imagery. Who hasn't daydreamed of perfectly executing an important skill in a critical situation? Imagery involves visualizing events in our mind's eye to recall or create our own experiences or to imitate others. Successful athletes purposefully use imagery to enhance performance. Imagery can be used to learn and practice skills, overcome technique problems, control performance anxiety, increase self-confidence, prepare for competition, and recreate success experiences. Imagery is best used with other mental skills (e.g., relaxation, positive self-talk, and goal setting) over a period of time to enhance performance.

There are three keys to effective imagery. First, imagery should be positive. Always visualize yourself performing correctly. When using imagery to correct problems, always follow a "replay" of your poor performance with an image of yourself overcoming the error and correctly executing the skill. Imagery builds muscle memory; positive imagery reinforces the memory of proper execution.

Second, imagery should involve as many senses as possible including visual, auditory (sounds), olfactory (smells), gustatory (taste), tactile (touch), kinesthetic (the feel of the body as it moves), and the emotions associated with the experience (e.g., satisfaction, pride). Kinesthetic sense is critical to successful imagery. Using many senses creates more vivid images; the more vivid the image, the more effective the imagery. When athletes engage in vivid imagery, their brain interprets these images as identical to actually performing the behavior.

You can improve the vividness and controllability of your images with systematic practice. Make imagery an integral part of your game. When first starting, keep the imagery concise and simple. Initially choose a skill that is easy to visualize. As you become more proficient, use imagery with more complex situations. Imagery is a supplement to physical practice that can provide an edge in competition. Imagery can be a useful substitution for physical practice when athletes are unable (e.g. fatigue, injury, or just too busy) to get to the practice court or field.

A third key to imagery is the perspective from which you "view" the image. An internal perspective means the athlete sees the image from behind their own eyes as if they were inside their bodies. An external perspective is one in which the athlete sees the image from outside their bodies as with watching a videotape. Elite athletes practice imagery from an internal perspective, which helps them become more aware of how the body feels when executing a skill. An external perspective also can be useful, for example, to enhance confidence if used to see oneself successfully performing in a tough situation.

When is the most effective time to use imagery? Imagery should be practiced systematically and regularly. Incorporate imagery before, during, and after each practice session. For closed skills such as pitching, serving, free throw shooting, high jump or long jump, or hitting a golf ball, imagery should be an important component of your pre-execution routine. After you have analyzed the situation and determined how to respond, visualize yourself correctly executing the skill. Likewise, following each performance, reinforce good plays by repeating them through imagery and correct any errors by visualizing yourself correctly executing the skill.

Imagery is a basic skill to include in your mental skills toolbox. With practice, imagery is a skill you can develop and use in different contexts to create and recreate success in your mind that subsequently will enhance your performance in competition.

Key Concepts for Imagery

Mental Rehearsal should be positive, vivid, and realistic. Try to use as many of your senses as you can in your imagery (sight, sound, movement, touch, smell, and emotions). Your imagery builds muscle memory/automaticity, so be sure to use *positive* imagery and see yourself performing well.

Mental rehearsal can build muscle memory. Visualizing perfect performance helps build automaticity and muscle memory for that performance. It is important to see yourself performing well. Replaying mistakes or poor performance over and over again in your mind likewise builds muscle memory – but, it is memory for what you want to avoid, similar to negative self-talk. Accordingly, you should follow any replay of an error with mentally rehearsing/seeing yourself perfectly performing the same skill in the same situation. We cannot expect perfection in our actual performance, but we can control our visualization so that we can rehearse perfectly and make it more likely we will perform well in the future.

Mental rehearsal can build confidence. The last time the Western Kentucky University men's basketball team advanced to the NCAA Sweet Sixteen, it was on a buzzer beater 3-point shot by Ty Rogers. After the game when the press asked Ty if he was nervous, he replied that he was not nervous because he had seen himself making that game winning shot thousands of times – in his own mind. Ty had use imagery to mentally rehearse being cool and confident in a tough situation and coming through for his team. If you visualize yourself performing perfectly a thousand times, when you are confronted with the real thing, you will bring that mentally rehearsed confidence to help you perform well in actual competition.

Mental rehearsal can help you problem solve for difficult situations. If you ever have thoughts of "What if [this bad thing happens]?" you can determine the best way to handle this situation, then visualize yourself dealing successfully with whatever challenge you may face. In the future, should this challenge present itself, you have the solution, you have practiced it (mentally), and you should be able to successfully overcome the challenge. (Also see Chapter 5 on Problem Solving.)

Mental rehearsal enables you to practice and perfect performance in competition. Olympic gold medalist swimmer Claire Donahue used a real-time audio recording to guide her through mentally rehearsing her pre-swim routine and her actual swim. At least two weeks before a big meet, Claire would spend 20 to 30 minutes a day mentally rehearsing her swim. If she was familiar with the pool and natatorium, she would incorporate that into her imagery. By the time she got to the meet, she was very comfortable with the surroundings and her swim in the competition pool. You can use imagery to mentally rehearse challenging situations to help ensure you are comfortable and prepared to meet those challenges when they occur.

Chapter 4 Exercises and Techniques

Being in a relaxed state is helpful for imagery. Thus, it is recommended that you review Chapter 6 on Relaxation before practicing imagery. If you are new to imagery, start with simple exercises and then progress to the more challenging visualization exercises. I recommend using the Imagery Rating Scale (see exercise sheet 4.1a) to track the quality of your imagery. Be sure to date the rating sheet so you can see how you are progressing in developing imagery skills. As you complete the imagery exercises, it may be helpful to have a friend read the exercise aloud while you practice the visualizing. Another option is to audio record the exercise and play it back for yourself as you work to develop your imagery skill.

Exercise 4.1: The Imagery Rating Scale

The most effective imagery is vivid and involves as many senses as possible including visual (sights), auditory (sounds), olfactory (smells), gustatory (taste), tactile (touch), kinesthetic (the feel of the body as it moves), and the emotions associated with the experience (e.g., satisfaction, pride, confidence). Rating the quality of your imagery will enable you to track your progress in developing imagery skills and will direct you to aspects of your imagery that may need more attention. Record comments to note what part of your visualization is working particularly well or that you need to work on in future imagery sessions. Summing the ratings for each aspect of the imagery will provide an index of the overall quality of your imagery. Total ratings can range from 0 (no image at all across all senses) to 21 (very realistic, strong, and clear images across all senses).

After your visualization, rate the quality of your imagery using the following scale.

3 – I could control the image; this sense was very realistic, strong, and clear
2 – I had some control over the image; this sense was moderately strong and clear
1 – I had little control over the image; this sense was not strong or clear
0 – This sense was not present; I was not able to evoke this sense in my image.

You can use exercise sheet 4.1a for this.

You can use this exercise sheet in conjunction with **Exercise 4.1: The Imagery Rating Scale**.

Exercise sheet 4.1a

IMAGERY RATING SCALE		
Focus of Imagery: _____	Date:	
Rate the degree to which you:	**Rating**	**Comments**
Saw the image (sight)		
Heard sounds (auditory)		
Smelled odors or fragrances (olfactory)		
Tasted flavors (gustatory)		
Felt what you touched (touch)		
Felt your body part(s) as it moved (kinesthetic)		
Felt emotions		
Total		

Read through **Exercise 4.1: The Imagery Rating Scale**. Before completing exercise sheet 4.1a, look through the example answers that follow.

Example 1: Using the Imagery Rating Scale for Seeing and Biting into a Lemon

Close your eyes and try to see a bright yellow lemon. Hold the lemon in your hand. Feel the texture of the lemon peel. Smell the sour lemon smell. Turn the lemon over in your hand and notice that a wedge of lemon has been cut out of the whole lemon. See yourself holding the wedge of lemon in your hand, moving it toward your mouth. Smell the fresh lemon juice. Take a bite of the lemon wedge. Feel your lips pucker and your mouth start to water as you taste the strong sour lemon taste. Now, slowly open your eyes, rest for a moment, then rate your visualization using the Imagery Rating Scale.

After your visualization, rate the quality of your imagery using the following scale.

3 – I could control the image; this sense was very realistic, strong, and clear
2 – I had some control over the image; this sense was moderately strong and clear
1 – I had little control over the image; this sense was not strong or clear
0 – This sense was not present; I was not able to evoke this sense in my image.

IMAGERY RATING SCALE		
Focus of Imagery: Seeing and tasting a lemon	**Date:** March 2, 2020	
Rate the degree to which you:	**Rating**	**Comments**
Saw the image (sight)	3	I could clearly see the lemon
Heard sounds (auditory)	0	I did not hear anything
Smelled odors or fragrances (olfactory)	1	I barely smelled the lemon
Tasted flavors (gustatory)	3	My mouth watered and I could taste the sour taste of lemon
Felt what you touched (touch)	2	I could feel texture of the lemon peel
Felt your body part(s) as it moved (kinesthetic)	1	I barely felt my hand and arm move as I moved the lemon
Felt emotions	3	The sour taste was really strong and I did not like it
Total	13	Overall, not a bad score because my visual and taste sensations were good. I need to work on the kinesthetic more.

Example 2: Using the Imagery Rating Scale for Closed-Space Dribbling in Soccer

Much of the time soccer players find themselves in a tight space from which they have to figure a way out. This is an example of using imagery to be creative and use different surfaces of the feet to dribble out of a closed space.

Close your eyes and try to see an image of you (a soccer player) dribbling the soccer ball using all surfaces of your feet, with quick touches to guide the ball in a controlled pattern around defenders. See your feet as you dribble the ball, hear the sound of your foot against the ball with each dribble; taste sweat as it drips down your face and into your mouth; smell the grass and the sweat of other players; and feel excited as you successfully dribble the ball around your opponents. Slowly open your eyes, rest a moment, then rate the quality of your visualization.

After your visualization, rate the quality of your imagery using the following scale.

3 – I could control the image; this sense was very realistic, strong, and clear

2 – I had some control over the image; this sense was moderately strong and clear

1 – I had little control over the image; this sense was not strong or clear

0 – This sense was not present; I was not able to evoke this sense in my image.

IMAGERY RATING SCALE		
Focus of Imagery: closed-space dribbling	**Date:** August 16, 2020	
Rate the degree to which you:	**Rating**	**Comments**
Saw the image (sight)	3	I could clearly see myself dribbling around opponents
Heard sounds (auditory)	2	I heard my foot make contact with the ball
Smelled odors or fragrances (olfactory)	1	I could smell that sweaty smell of hot athletes, but not much
Tasted flavors (gustatory)	1	I tried to taste the sweat on my face, but it was not strong
Felt what you touched (touch)	2	I felt my foot make contact with the ball when I made quick touches to guide the ball.
Felt your body part(s) as it moved (kinesthetic)	2	I could somewhat feel my legs moving to make contact with the ball and running down the field
Felt emotions	2	I was concentrating and felt pretty good about my performance.
Total	13	This was a difficult scenario to visualize. I am getting better and this is helping me when I am actually on the field with the ball.

Exercise 4.2: Images for Basic Senses

Remember to begin each exercise in a relaxed state and to complete the Imagery Rating Scale after your imagery practice (you can use exercise sheet 4.1a for this). This exercise is not sport specific, but will help you develop your imagery skills for each of the human senses. Your ratings will inform you about which senses you may need to practice.

Vision. Close your eyes and try to see a red rose. Focus on the red color of the petals and the green stem. Now, change the color of the rose to a deep yellow rose. Now, try to see the rose go back to a deep red. Now, replace the rose with a banana. Do you see the yellow of the banana peel? Can you form an image of a round orange? Can you change the image of the orange into a bright red apple?

Sound. Close your eyes and try to hear the sound of heavy rain on the roof. Can you hear a thunder clap in the distance and now one much closer? Think of the fight song for your school. Can you hear the band playing the fight song? Can you hear the ring tone on your phone?

Kinesthetic. Close your eyes and try to feel the tension on your arms when you lift a heavy object such as your backpack full of books. Try to feel the sensation in your legs when you walk up several flights of stairs. How does this feel different from walking up the same stairs after a demanding workout? Try to feel that heaviness in your legs as they move up the stairs. Don't move your head, but try to feel how it feels when you nod your head up and down to signal yes.

Touch. Close your eyes and try to feel the fuzzy surface of a peach. Notice how it feels like velvet. Contrast this feeling with the fuzzy but rougher surface of a tennis ball. Now try to feel the pebbled, leathery texture of a basketball, the dimpled texture and hard surface of a golf ball, the smooth but sectioned surface of a volleyball or soccer ball, and the leather surface and seams of a baseball or softball.

Smell. Close your eyes and try to smell fresh baked cookies, the sweet fragrance of a rose, the putrid smell of sour milk, the smell of your favorite perfume or cologne, the chlorine smell of a swimming pool, and the summer smell of freshly cut grass.

Taste. Close your eyes and try to taste the sugary taste of a fresh cinnamon roll, the taste of rich chocolate melting on your tongue, the salty taste of sweat as it slips into your mouth during hard exercise, and the sour taste of a fresh lemon.

Exercise 4.3: Sport-Specific Images

Remember to begin each exercise in a relaxed state and to complete the Imagery Rating Scale after your imagery practice (you can use exercise sheet 4.1a for this). This exercise is sport specific and will help you develop your imagery skills for your sport. The imagery scripts here start with simple imagery tasks and progress to more complex images. Some athletes find it helpful to develop an imagery script to help them prepare for specific situations in their sport (e.g., an important game/match/meet) or specific skills they are developing. The script can be audio recorded and played back to guide the imagery session. Remember to use positive imagery and see yourself being successful in executing your skills.

Script 1: Equipment

Close your eyes and visualize a key piece of equipment from your sport. This might be the ball you use in your sport, swimming goggles, track shoes, etc. Using imagery, hold this equipment in your hand. Notice its weight, its texture, and the feel of the material it is made of. Bring the equipment closer to your nose. Can you smell the leather or rubber or wood? Lower the equipment so that you can clearly see it. What color is it? Is it new or worn? Does it have a manufacturer's label on it? Now drop the equipment to the floor. What sound do you hear as it hits the floor? Pick the equipment up and hold it as though preparing to use it. Slowly open your eyes and rate your imagery.

Script 2: Your Practice Area

Close your eyes and visualize where you normally practice. This may be a court, a field, a pool, or some other area. Look around and scan the area. What do you see? Notice the size of the area, the smells, and the sounds. Try to see the area as if you are there waiting to practice. Can you see your coach preparing for practice? Teammates? Slowly open your eyes and rate your imagery.

Script 3: Specific Skill

Close your eyes and see yourself performing a specific skill in your sport (e.g., serving, hitting, throwing, starting, shooting, dribbling, etc.). Go through the performance from start to finish. Try to feel the muscles in your arms and legs as you perform this skill. Try to see yourself as you would if you were actually performing this skill. How does it feel as you contact the ball (or the water, etc.)? See yourself performing this skill perfectly. Perform the skill again and again, each time executing perfectly and building confidence in performing this skill. Focus on the different feel of your muscles as your perform various components of this skill. Once you have completed the performance, slowly open your eyes and rate your imagery.

Note: It is helpful to identify the keys to successfully performing your skill and incorporate the keys into a personal imagery script, as in the example that follows for hitting a volleyball. Ask your coach for help identifying the keys to performing your important component skills.

Example Script for Specific Skill of Hitting in Volleyball

Close your eyes and see the volleyball court from your position on the court. See the setter set the ball for you. Think of the performance keys and use your hitting triggers/cues: Be Late, Wait and Accelerate. Reach with your drive step. Elbow up early. In the "finish" portion of your swing, keep your elbow above your ear. Make a big circle. Stay open to your primary shot and go through your progression. See yourself execute a perfect swing and score a kill. Slowly open your eyes and rate your image.

Script 4: Putting It All Together

Close your eyes and see yourself in the setting where you compete. Look around and notice your teammates finishing their warmups and the coach on the side. Notice the competition also warming up. See the crowd gathering for the start of the competition. As you step onto the court/field/track/deck, you feel a bit anxious, so you take several deep slow breaths and relax. Now you feel calm, focused, and ready to perform. See yourself in competition performing very well, executing perfectly. Notice the sensations in your body as your move, the sounds you hear, and the positive emotions you feel as you do very well in this competition. Your coach and teammates are pleased. Hear the crowd as they cheer for you. Slowly open your eyes and rate your image.

Note: Incorporating elements specific to your sport and to your situation will help make the imagery more vivid. Use terminology, equipment, skills, and actual competitors specific to you to make your imagery more effective. As you improve your imagery skills, you can develop more complex visualization scripts to help you practice the skills and situations you find challenging.

Exercise 4.4: Fun with Imagery

The two exercises in this section (4.4a and 4.4b) are well known to sport psychologists and often are used to get buy-in from athletes for imagery use.

Exercise 4.4a: Arm as a Steel Bar

Perhaps the origin of this first exercise is in gymnastics where one of the more widely recognized strength elements on the rings is the iron cross, an element in which the gymnast, in mid-air, must extend his arms straight out from his body while holding the rings steady for at least two seconds. The gymnast is encouraged to imagine a steel bar extending from one hand, through his shoulders into the other hand. This image helps the gymnast have the strength and concentration to maintain the iron cross for the required duration.

The Arm as a Steel Bar exercise fairly quickly illustrates how imagery can be used to improve performance. It is a two-part exercise and requires a partner, preferably of approximately the same height and strength.

Step 1: The partners should face each other an arm's length apart. One partner (A) should extend his/her arm straight across placing the palm facing up on partner B's shoulder. Partner B should link his/her hands on the other's straight arm just above the elbow. Partner A should tighten his/her arm muscles to prevent partner B from bending his/her elbow while pulling down with hands clasped. Once done, partners should change positions and repeat.

Step 2: In this round, as s/he extends his/her arm, to increase strength, partner A should close his/her eyes and imagine a steel bar running from the fingertips of one hand, through the shoulders, to the fingertips of the other hand, all the way into the wall – such that the arm is as strong as the steel bar. Once the image is created (and maintained), partner B should again try to pull down with clasped hands to bend the elbow. In most cases, partner B has a more difficult time bending the elbow when the steel bar is visualized because the imagery has increased the strength of the arm. Partners should switch roles so each can experience the steel bar effect.

Note: This exercise illustrates how simple imagery can increase strength. When systematic imagery is used, it likewise can increase performance in competition.

Exercise 4.4: Fun with Imagery (cont.)

Exercise 4.4b: Ring on a String

Each athlete will need a length of string slightly longer than twice the length of the distance from their elbow to their fingertips, and a heavy bolt (available from any hardware store for about 25 cents). If the athlete has a championship ring, that will work in lieu of the bolt.

Thread the bolt through the string. Have each athlete place his/her elbows on a table (or on their knees if no table is available), and hold each end of the string lightly between the thumb and index finger so that the bolt is suspended on the string to form a triangle. Without moving the hand or fingers, have the athlete focus on the bolt and imagine the bolt swinging from side to side (like a clock pendulum). Some find it helpful to close their eyes, but it is not necessary. For most athletes, there will be some movement in the string. Next, the athlete can imagine the bolt moving forward and backward; then in a circle counter clockwise; then reverse to a clockwise circle. Most athletes are able to produce the desired movement without moving their hands/fingers, using only imagery. One team I work with uses visualization to see the bolt as a championship ring – which may be more likely in their future if athletes practice imagery to improve performance.

Note: This exercise illustrates imagery's ability to invoke subtle messages from the brain to neurons and muscles in the arms, hands, and fingers. These subtle impulses are what causes the string to move. This same process is what enables imagery to build motor memory for skills practiced through mental rehearsal.

Exercise 4.5: Using Imagery to Successfully Deal with Problem Situations

1. Identify between three and five competitive situations that are likely to cause you some difficulty.
2. Take one situation at a time. Briefly describe the situation.
3. Try to form a very graphic image of the situation. Include all the sensations you would experience – that is, the sights (e.g., the performance setting – field, court, pool, green – and the crowd, the ball, etc.); the sounds (e.g., noise from spectators, perhaps your heart beating rapidly, etc.); and the smells, the tactile sensations (e.g., the feel of your club in your hand, etc.) that you would experience in such a situation. Include self-talk that is likely to be occurring in this situation, that is, the thoughts that you are having as you evaluate the situation. Try to experience all of the sensations you would in an actual situation. Try to assume a first-person perspective in visualizing the situation.
4. Using imagery, see yourself using the techniques you have been practicing to handle the situation – that is, recognize what is going on "psychologically" – and use your mental skills to deal effectively with the situation so that you perform successfully.

For each situation you identified, visualize yourself doing the following:

1. **Using your positive self-talk skills** to:
   a. RECOGNIZE that you are engaging in negative self-talk,
   b. STOP the negative self-talk, and
   c. REPLACE the negative self-talk with positive self-talk.
      In particular, especially if the situation is following poor execution, remember to focus on the PRESENT (not the past – it cannot be changed), the POSITIVE (the correct performance you want to accomplish), and PERFORMANCE (repeat to yourself the proper execution you want to accomplish).
2. **Recognizing feelings of anxiety.** Then using relaxation techniques to gain your composure and focus on the positive performance you know you can accomplish.
3. **Performing successfully in this difficult situation.** It is important to use imagery to execute in the imagery what you would like to accomplish on the course/court/ field, etc. Include in your imagery the positive feelings you experience after overcoming the difficult circumstances, feelings of satisfaction and accomplishment as well as a feeling of confidence in your ability to deal with the situation.

The more you use mental practice to overcome such situations, the stronger the "memory" for these success experiences. Mental rehearsal is one of the best ways to break the psychological habit of becoming anxious in less than perfect situations.

Every athlete executes poorly at some point and is going to have to deal with less than preferred situations. You become conditioned in terms of your dominant response. If your past pattern has been to become anxious and "choke," you need to break this pattern. Mental rehearsal can enable you to break the negative pattern of responding. Your mind does not distinguish between memories of actual past events and imagined events in terms of building the dominant response. The bottom line is to rehearse success (whether actually or through imagery) so often that confidence becomes the dominant response. Imagery is very helpful because by controlling the image, you can always have a success experience – even in the most difficult situations. Success experiences, actual or mentally rehearsed, are great for building confidence!

Problem Solving and Continuous Learning to Build Resilience

5

Without a doubt, situations will arise where you will be confronted with unexpected challenges. Some of these challenges will be minor (e.g., broken shoe lace) and others will be more demanding (e.g., failure of a key piece of equipment). Problem solving is more difficult if there is high risk (e.g., lives are at stake), time pressure (i.e., how quickly a decision must be made), uncertain goals (i.e., the correct solution is not clear), ambiguous or incomplete information (i.e., inferences must be made to best interpret relevant factors), and teamwork is required (i.e., a coordinated effort is needed to successfully resolve the problem).

When we are faced with a challenge, the flight-or-fight part of our brain takes over and can make us feel uncomfortable. You need to recognize that some discomfort or unease is natural when we are faced with an important decision. Rather than thinking of this discomfort as something to avoid, learn to change your reaction to the situation to one in which you view pressure as something you can accept and deal with, or even welcome. Practicing under pressure will help you learn to deal with unanticipated problems or pressure situations that arise. One method for learning to deal with high pressure competitive situations is to create high pressure practices (e.g., run a lap for each free throw you miss) and then focus on acclimating to and feeling comfortable with the pressure as much as developing the skilled performance.

Athletes need to develop the skill of learned resourcefulness, the ability to combine many of the skills in your mental skills toolbox to solve problems, to adjust and adapt to stressful situations, and to perform well under pressure. Important skills include: (1) positive self-talk to focus on the desired solution to your problem, your area of impact, what you can do; (2) self-regulation of emotions with techniques such as relaxation to calm your mind so that you can process information accurately and feel in control; (3) perspective to recognize that most situations in sports are not life or death situations even if they hold great importance for the athlete; and (4) confidence to recognize that you can successfully solve most problems. Learned resourcefulness is foundational for resilience. Resilience is the ability to adjust and adapt, to bounce back from errors and difficulties, and to overcome the challenges that will confront each of us.

A key to resilience is viewing challenges, errors, and difficult situations as learning experiences that develop learned resourcefulness. In the military, the process of reviewing and reflecting on performance is termed an "After Action Review" and is required after important strategic missions. This structured review evaluates the outcome of the mission, what led to success/failure, and how performance can be improved the next time out. Thus, the review is proactive focusing on improvement in the future; it is not blaming or punitive for past performance. The After Action Review can be extremely useful for athletes to learn from past performance.

Mental Skills: Error-Based Learning

By nature, athletes are competitive and do not like to make mistakes. In fact, the desire for excellent performance is what drives many athletes. How one responds to mistakes and errors is an important determinant in whether the athlete's performance over the long term will develop and improve or will deteriorate. Making errors and learning to correct errors is key in developing problem solving skills. Dealing with failure, facing challenges, and correcting mistakes are essential for developing resilience, which is foundational to mental toughness. Athletes who experience errors and discover how to recover from them learn that success is possible even subsequent to making an error. The ability to adapt, adjust, and overcome difficulty is the hallmark of resilience.

The perspective of viewing an error as a beneficial opportunity to learn – not only how to correct the mistake but also how to avoid the problem in the future – is key to developing problem solving skills. Errors can reflect incorrect assumptions by the athlete about his/her performance that can be corrected in subsequent performance. Making errors and discovering how to correct them enables the athlete to learn error-management strategies that help identify possible types of errors and how to prevent different types of errors in the future.

Reflect on a situation that is particularly challenging for you, when you are more likely to make an error. What are the aspects of the situation that you can control (e.g., positive self-talk, relaxation, attitude, timing, response choice, skill execution, etc.)? These are the keys to a problem-solving strategy. Use your own judgment and that of your coach to develop a plan to perform well in this situation. You can use imagery to rehearse dealing with this challenge to increase confidence in your ability to perform successfully in this difficult situation.

Athletes make errors. Many sport statistics are expressed in terms of percentage of successful execution relative to percentage of errors – clearly indicating that errors happen. When an athlete makes an error, corrects the error, and persists to complete a task or competition successfully, s/he learns that s/he can rebound and perform well despite having committed an error. An athlete that has never made an error in practice will be unable to correct errors in competition. Thus, there is some concern for young athletes who are protected from failure/making errors and deprived of the opportunity to learn how to rebound after committing an error.

When an athlete is preparing for a big event (e.g., conference tournament, regionals, Olympics, etc.), every event up to that big, target event should be considered a learning opportunity. Whether the athlete performs well or poorly, there are lessons to be learned that can be critical for optimal performance during the big event. After an event, the athlete should record what went well and why and, importantly, what did not go well and what needs to be done to improve performance. It is important to write down this information very shortly after the event while the performance is still fresh in the athlete's memory. This record will prove invaluable in preparing for the next competition. Accumulated records will be quite informative in preparing for "the big event" to track progress and ensure the athlete is prepared to prevent or overcome past errors. It is important to get the coach's perspective after each event to confirm the perceptions of the athlete in terms of both the performance and how to improve the performance. This is especially true when there are not objective indicators of performance (i.e., Were skill components executed correctly? Was the correct strategy used? etc.). The athlete needs to learn what caused the error and how it can be avoided in the future.

Although competitive athletes do not like to commit errors, it is important for an athlete to view errors as a learning experience to inform future performance. After the competition is over is the time to review, reflect, reinforce good performance, and correct poor performance. During the competition, the athlete should stay fully focused on the Present Positive Performance needed for success. The time for analysis is when "the shoes are off" – that is, after the competition is over.

Key Concepts for Problem Solving and Continuous Learning

Problems will arise. Difficult situations provide important learning opportunities. Recognize that some discomfort is normal when facing challenges and difficult situations. Likewise, recognize that you have a toolbox of mental skills to help you deal with these situations. Learn to be resourceful and gain confidence when you use mental skills such as positive self-talk, self-regulation of emotions, and perspective to successfully learn from your successes and, especially, to learn from your failures to deal with challenging situations. Continuous learning is the key to becoming more resilient and more resourceful so that you can successfully meet increasingly difficult challenges.

Chapter 5 Exercises and Techniques

To develop resilience and learned resourcefulness, it is important to adopt a learning mindset – the belief that we should continue to learn from our experiences to become more intelligent about our sport and that we can continue to develop the skills we need to succeed. Challenges and failures are opportunities to improve, and provide important information to guide our learning. If we work hard and persevere in the face of adversity, we become more resilient; this, in turn, increases our confidence that we can deal successfully with challenges, and ultimately enables us to deal successfully with the most challenging situations.

Exercise 5.1: Review and Reflect for Continuous Learning

In the military, the process of reviewing and reflecting on performance is termed an "After Action Review" and is required after important strategic missions. This structured review evaluates the outcome of the mission, what led to success/failure, and how performance can be improved the next time out. The After Action Review can be extremely useful for athletes to learn from past performance.

Learning from practice. Some athletes dread practice; however, successful athletes consider every practice to be a learning opportunity. An Olympic gold medalist said: "Competition will be here quicker than you think. You need to take advantage of every opportunity you have to appreciate and enjoy practice." Most coaches carefully plan practice sessions to ensure their athletes develop the skills they need to be successful in competition. If you want to get the most out of your practice time, in addition to being fully engaged during practice, after practice reflect on the day's workout, then record what you did well and what you need to focus on to improve.

Learning from competition. A competition provides a unique learning experience that practice sessions cannot provide – because it is the actual competition. Athletes devote many hours preparing for competition and should use every competition as a learning opportunity. After each competition, reflect on your performance. Consider what you did well and why. Importantly, consider what you did *not* do well and why. The answers to the latter questions will provide valuable information to guide your practice so that next competition you can improve your performance.

Note: You can use exercise sheet 5.1a, which is an example of a generic worksheet, to review and reflect on practice or competition. The more you adapt the worksheet to be specific to your sport and to your personal performance goals, the more helpful it will be in providing information to guide your personal improvement plan.

You can use this exercise sheet in conjunction with **Exercise 5.1: Review and Reflect for Continuous Learning**. It is a generic worksheet that you can adapt to suit your own needs.

Exercise sheet 5.1a

REVIEW AND REFLECT WORKSHEET

Event: _____ (specific competition or practice)

Date: _____

A. My personal goal for this event:

Performance evaluation relative to goal:

B. Lessons learned:

1.

2.

3.

C. Evaluate component skills key to my performance:

Skill 1 _____
Evaluation:

Skill 2 _____
Evaluation:

Skill 3 _____
Evaluation:

D. Additional comments/lessons learned (*write on back of this sheet, if needed*)

Read through **Exercise 5.1: Review and Reflect for Continuous Learning**, use exercise sheet 5.1a (adapted to fit your needs), then look through the blank worksheet that follows, which has been adapted to suit the needs of a swimmer attending a meet.

REVIEW AND REFLECT WORKSHEET

Event: _____ (specific competition or practice)

Date: _____

A. Personal goals for event

Goal: Go a good time: _____ or better Actual time: _____

Goal: Place in the top _____   Place: _____

Comments:

B. Lessons learned from the meet

Use visualization

Practice: Tues   Wed   Thurs   Fri   Sat

Comments:

C. Evaluate swim components

Skill 1: Underwaters

Number of kicks off each wall: _____ Start _____ W2 _____ W3 _____ W4

Skill 2: Size and speed

#Kicks: _____ Lap 1 _____ Lap 2 _____ Lap 3 _____ Lap 4

Accelerate: _____% of 100m accelerating

Kick kick: _____% of 100m Kick-kicking

Turns (time): _____ Turn 1 _____ Turn 2 _____ Turn 3

D. Additional comments/lessons learned

Read through **Exercise 5.1: Review and Reflect for Continuous Learning**, before completing exercise sheet 5.1a (adapted to suit your needs), look through the worksheet below completed by a golfer.

REVIEW AND REFLECT WORKSHEET

Event: Tournament at Eastside Country Club
Date: April 6-8

A. Goals for this event: Score < 80 on each round
Fewer than 3 3-putts per round
Performance evaluation relative to goal: Scored 80, 82, and 77
Total of 12 3-putts across 3 rounds

B. Lessons learned:

1. I was distracted by the crowd on several greens; this resulted in poor putting. I need to work on blocking out the crowd and focusing on my putting.
2. I forgot to use my routine on a number of my drives. Using my routine and repeating my swing thought to myself seemed to work. I need to do this every hole.
3. My approach shot was working well. I was happy with the number of greens I made in regulation.

C. Evaluate component skills key to my performance
Skill 1: Drive
Evaluation: I wasn't hitting the ball well off the tee. Number of fairways hit was way off – I hit the fringe close to a third of the time.

Skill 2: Approach shots
Evaluation: All of my practice on the short game paid off. I did well in hitting greens in regulation.

Skill 3: Putting
Evaluation: I putted pretty well when I focused and used my putting performance cue. I did not meet my goal for putting.

D. Additional comments/lessons learned
Using routines is really helpful for my game. I hit much better on the holes I remembered to use my routine.
I need to practice reading greens with different types of grass (e.g., Rye, Bermuda, Bentgrass).

Exercise 5.2: Dealing with the "What Ifs"

In anticipation of a big competition, many athletes start to worry and think "What if [this happens]?" Even though the "What ifs" are common, they are negative self-talk and are detrimental to performance. If the "What ifs" are viewed within a problem-solving context, they can be used to build confidence in your ability to address the challenges that will inevitably arise. Working through the "What ifs," determining the best way to deal with the problem should it happen, and then mentally rehearsing successfully handling the problem can create preparedness to deal with potential problem situations. Exercise sheet 5.2a will take you through this process. Think of this worksheet as something of a flowchart.

You can use this exercise sheet in conjunction with **Exercise 5.2: Dealing with the "What Ifs"**.

Exercise sheet 5.2a

"WHAT IFS" WORKSHEET

1. a. What is the worry? _____

    b. What if _____ happens?

    c. Is this a realistic concern? _____

    d. Has this happened before? _____

    e. How likely is it to happen? _____

2. a. If it is *not* likely to happen, then replace the "What if" worry with positive self-talk. Focus on what you can do to prepare for the competition.

    b. If this *is* a realistic concern, what is the most advantageous response if it does happen? _____

    (If you do not know, consult with your coach or trusted teammate.)

3. Once you have determined the best response in this situation:

    a. If possible, practice actually performing the desired response.

    b. Use imagery to mentally rehearse seeing yourself deal successfully with the situation.

    c. Develop an affirmation statement to capture the essence of the successful response.

    Affirmation Statement:

Read through **Exercise 5.2: Dealing with the "What Ifs"**, complete exercise sheet 5.2a, then look through the completed worksheet below, which uses the example of a basketball game.

"WHAT IFS" WORKSHEET

1. a. What is the worry? Being fouled.
   b. What if I am fouled in the final seconds of the game, we are down by one, and I miss the free throws?
   c. Is this a realistic concern? Yes
   d. Has this happened before? Yes
   e. How likely is it to happen?
      I am a key player and am likely to be in the game in the final seconds - so, it could happen.

2. a. If it is *not* likely to happen, then replace the "What if" worry with positive self-talk. Focus on what you can do to prepare for the competition.
   b. If this *is* a realistic concern, what is the most advantageous response if it does happen? The best response is to make the free throws despite the pressure.
      (If you do not know, consult with your coach or trusted teammate.)

3. Once you have determined the best response in this situation:
   a. If possible, practice actually performing the desired response.
      Increase the number of free throws I shoot and make in practice.
      • Check with the shot coach to ensure I am using the best technique.
      • Develop a routine for free throw shooting and use it for every free throw I shoot.
      • Create pressure in practice – for example, all of my teammates have to complete a suicide line drill for every free throw I miss.
   b. Use imagery to mentally rehearse seeing yourself deal successfully with the situation.
      I will visualize myself in the very situation I identified in my "What if" statement. I will see myself get fouled, go to the line in the high pressure situation, use my routine, and sink the free throws – nothing but net!
   c. Develop an affirmation statement to capture the essence of the successful response.
      Affirmation Statement: I am a great free throw shooter. I make pressure shots.

Part II

Mental Skills

B. The Body (Physiological Skills and the Mind–Body Connection)

Relaxation, Controlling Performance Anxiety, and Mindfulness

6

We experience stress when we are confronted with a situation that we cannot control. As mentioned in the introduction to this book, there are many things we cannot control in a competitive situation. Thus, most athletes experience at least some performance anxiety, a natural response to a situation in which one hopes to perform well but is unable to control all aspects of the situation. Learning to control anxiety will lead to increased confidence and better performance.

When we encounter a stressful situation, our bodies automatically react with both physical and psychological responses. These responses are driven by our sympathetic nervous system, a part of the autonomic nervous system that controls the unconscious physical functions in our body. The sympathetic nervous system is activated when we feel threatened and can cause the heart to race, blood vessels to constrict, muscles to tense, eyes to dilate, shallow breathing, goose bumps, and/or sweating. Psychological responses include a narrowing of attention, an internal focus of attention, perception of time speeding up leading to rushing performance, and a deterioration in the ability to process information. An optimal level of arousal is needed for effective performance. When we are anxious, it is detrimental to our performance. Thus, we need to learn to control the competitive anxiety we experience to ensure that we are physically ready to perform.

Mental Skills: Relaxation and Control of Physiological Arousal

The ability to focus is an important mental skill for an athlete in a competitive situation. The athlete must be able to concentrate on relevant aspects of the situation and block out distracting, irrelevant information. The component skills involved in a winning focus include attentional skills, self-talk, and control of physiological arousal. Attentional skills include the ability to focus solely on the relevant aspects of the immediate competitive situation. Self-talk refers to what we tell ourselves about the situation. Control of physiological arousal refers to the ability to detect and release tension.

Control of physiological arousal is key in developing confidence. The mind and the body are inextricably connected. The mind influences the body and the body influences the mind. When competing, athletes should be up for the competition but not so aroused that it hinders their performance. Individuals differ in their optimal level of arousal for competition. When that optimal level is surpassed, the athlete develops physiological reactions that can interfere with performance. When an athlete experiences "butterflies" in the stomach, tension in the shoulders, and sweaty palms, it signals to our mind that we are anxious; this may lead to performance errors. Errors, in turn, cause us to begin to doubt our ability to play well, which may cause us to become more tense and anxious leading to more errors. This sequence triggers the downward spiral that is so detrimental to performance. In addition, anxiety may cause the athlete's focus to narrow and become inflexible causing the athlete to miss important information in the environment (e.g., coach's instructions, location of teammates or competitors, etc.).

Anxious feelings and thoughts are normal reactions to competitive stress and are experienced by most athletes. Successful competitive athletes learn to recognize and control their level of physical tension. Some athletes may recognize competitive anxiety and tell themselves to "relax." However, unless the athlete knows specific relaxation techniques, this well-meaning advice may only cause more anxiety. Learning to recognize and control competitive stress is an important mental skill for every athlete.

Instructions are readily available for progressive relaxation, a technique that focuses on reducing the physiological arousal experienced by the athlete. Progressive relaxation involves first contracting and then relaxing various muscle groups to help us identify the differences between feelings of tension and relaxation. This contrast and comparison enables the athlete to detect muscle tension when it occurs and to reduce the tension through a specific relaxation technique targeting the tense areas of the body. Eliminating physiological tension, particularly when paired with positive self-talk, breaks the downward spiral. We replace tension with relaxed confidence that signals our mind that we are relaxed and ready to perform. Another useful, easily implemented technique for relaxation is one-breath relaxation. Simply breathe in very slowly to a count of three to five, hold this breath for the same length of time, then exhale just as slowly while relaxing. Do this three times and you should feel more relaxed.

Each athlete must find his/her optimal level of arousal, which lies somewhere between being completely relaxed (e.g., sleep) and over aroused (e.g., agitated, nervous). The zone of optimal arousal is a function of the individual, the sport, and the situation. Some sports require low levels of arousal (e.g., target shooting) and some require a high degree of arousal (e.g., powerlifting). Most sports fall somewhere in between. As the level of arousal moves out of the optimal zone in either direction, performance deteriorates. If we are too relaxed, we miss important information in the competitive context and are slow to respond. If we are over aroused, our attention narrows, we again miss important information, and are unable to think flexibly. Some athletes need to pump themselves up before competing while others need to calm themselves down. The key is to find your optimal level and to control your level of arousal so that you are in control of the situation.

In sum, the ability to recognize and control physiological arousal is an important mental skill for the competitive athlete. When the athlete is able to recognize tension or other detrimental forms of arousal (e.g., sweaty palms, trembling hands, etc.) and then control arousal level through relaxation techniques, it sends an important message to the mind: "I am calm, cool, collected, in control, and ready to compete." This results in positive self-talk and enhanced confidence, putting the athlete in a better mindset to perform well on the court/field and enhancing performance.

Mental Skills: Mindfulness

Mindfulness is quite popular, almost faddish. If you were to click on 20 sites from a Google search on "mindfulness," chances are you would find 20 different definitions of mindfulness. Mindfulness is a combination of several mental skills, the two most important being relaxation and concentration. Mindfulness is a state in which an individual purposefully focuses on targeted aspects of the present and fully accepts, without judgment or evaluation, the emotions s/he is experiencing. One may engage in mindfulness for less than a minute, several minutes, or even longer.

Mindfulness may be as simple as taking several deep, slow breaths to relax and block distractions and other thoughts from your mind while focusing on how your body feels as you breathe; note how your chest rises and falls, how your lungs expand and contract; be fully present in the moment thinking only of your own breathing. If your mind wanders from your breathing, gently redirect your attention to your breath.

Many benefits have been attributed to mindfulness including: reduced stress and anxiety, improved working memory, better focus and ability to block out distractions, decreased emotional reactivity, more flexible thinking, and less negative thinking. Mindfulness can improve mood by enabling us to let go of negative thoughts (e.g., to stop replaying mistakes over and over again in our mind) by focusing only on the present. This process helps us regulate our emotions.

Practicing mindfulness can help us accept some of the negative emotions that we experience, which can put us in a better mindset to deal with challenging situations in a constructive manner. Mindfulness, like any other mental skill, must be practiced to experience its benefits.

Key Concepts in Relaxation, Controlling Performance Anxiety, and Mindfulness

Feelings of stress, anxiety, and tension are natural reactions to challenging situations. When we are able to recognize tension and other physical signs of anxiety and are able to control our level of physical arousal, it sends an important message to our brain that we are in control of the situation. This, in turn, helps to reduce stress and anxiety and helps us perform well in challenging situations. A simple deep breathing exercise can help us gain control and relax physically.

Each athlete must find his/her optimal level of arousal. The optimal level of arousal for an individual is a function of the individual, the sport, and the situation. The key is to be able to control your level of arousal so that you take in appropriate information, flexibly process this information, and be in control of your response to the situation.

Mindfulness is a practice that can help us control our thoughts to block out distractions and to focus fully on the present. Mindfulness involves relaxation and purposeful attention to the present while accepting the thoughts and emotions we are experiencing.

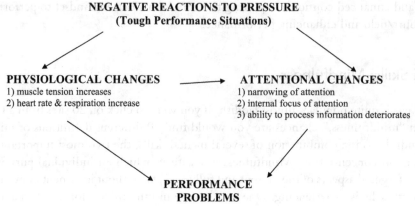

NEGATIVE REACTIONS TO PRESSURE
(Tough Performance Situations)

PHYSIOLOGICAL CHANGES
1) muscle tension increases
2) heart rate & respiration increase

ATTENTIONAL CHANGES
1) narrowing of attention
2) internal focus of attention
3) ability to process information deteriorates

PERFORMANCE
PROBLEMS
- disturbances in muscle coordination & timing
- rushing (perception of time is sped up)
- inability to attend to task relevant cues
- fatigue and muscle tightness

TO DEAL WITH PRESSURE
- Identify specific situations – develop a coping plan including mental skills.
- Control physiological arousal with relaxation techniques.
- Control concentration/attention.
- Focus on Positive, Present, Performance (not the outcome; not the past).
- Use centering (relaxed, focused).

Figure 6.1 Physical and psychological effects of stress

Chapter 6 Exercises and Techniques

Exercise 6.1: Deep Breathing to Release Tension and Relax

Deep breathing is an effective and straightforward technique to release tension and to relax. This type of breathing is known as rhythmic breathing, diaphragmatic breathing, abdominal breathing, belly breathing, deep breathing, or relaxation breathing. Depending on the teacher and the context (e.g., sports, dance, yoga), the exercise may vary and may emphasize different parts of the body, including the abdomen, the diaphragm, and the chest. Even with many variations, taking in a deep slow breath, holding it for the same length of time, then slowly exhaling generally has a calming and relaxing effect. The following are simple directions for deep breathing. Although easily learned, deep breathing should be practiced regularly to ensure you are comfortable with it when you need it to relax prior to, or during, competition. Practicing deep breathing in pressure situations in practice, or any time you feel annoyed or irritated, will help demonstrate its effectiveness in reducing tension.

When first learning deep breathing, it is helpful to be in a quiet place. Sit up relatively straight in a comfortable chair with both feet on the floor. You should use a three- to six-count for all three parts of each deep breath. Start with a three-count; as you improve try to work up to a five- or six-count. Even a three-count will be effective in releasing tension. Once you are comfortable with deep breathing, you should be able to use it in virtually any situation to quickly release tension and relax.

Directions. Take in a deep, slow breath to a slow count of three. Feel your lungs filling up and expanding as you inhale. Hold this breath to a count of three. Then slowly, again to a count of three, exhale. Most individuals find a slow, steady exhale to be the most difficult part of this exercise. As you exhale, feel the tension release from your body. Repeating a cue word while you exhale (e.g., the word "relax" or "release," or "calm") will help condition your body to relax when you use the cue word later to trigger a relaxed state.

Again, count *one, two, three* as you slowly breathe in and feel your lungs expand. Count *one, two, three* as you hold this breath. Now, count *one, two, three* as you slowly exhale and feel the tension leave your body.

Now, a third time - count *one, two, three* as you slowly breathe in. Count *one, two, three* as you hold this breath. Now, using your cue word, count *relax, relax, relax* as you slowly exhale.

A fun variation of this script is to think of your favorite hot food (e.g., pie, soup, cookies, pizza) and substitute these directions for inhaling (smell) and exhaling (blow to cool): Smell the pie (*one, two, three*); enjoy (hold) the aroma (*one, two, three*); now, cool the pie (*one, two, three*).

Most people find that with one to three repetitions of a deep breath, they are quite relaxed. However, deep breathing may be repeated for a period of several minutes to gain a state of complete relaxation. For many closed skills (e.g., serving, shooting free throws or penalty shots, or hitting a golf ball), taking a single deep breath before execution of the skill calms the mind and improves performance.

Exercise 6.2: Tracking Your Relaxation

Tracking your body's response to relaxation will help you focus on the keys to relaxation and will enable you to see if you are becoming better at relaxation. Once you have developed the skill to relax easily, tracking your body's response will enable you to ensure your are maintaining an appropriate level of relaxation. The appropriate level of relaxation will differ depending on the individual and sport situation.

To complete the Pre-Relaxation and Post-Relaxation Questionnaires (exercise sheets 6.2a and 6.2b), read each question and answer honestly to indicate how you feel at the time. To get an overall score, first subtract your ratings for items 3, 4, and 5 from 6, then add these numbers with the ratings for items 1, 2, 6, 7, and 8.

Scores on the pre- and post-Relaxation Questionnaires can range from 8 to 40. The ability to lower your total score from the pre- to post-questionnaire is more important than the absolute value of your total score. It is very important to be honest when answering both the pre- and post-questionnaires. Examine the difference in your pre- and post-scores for the Relaxation Questionnaire and the difference between your pre- and post-rate for your heart rate. If your relaxation session was successful, both your questionnaire score and your heart rate should be lower after relaxing. A lower resting heart is one indication of a high level of cardiovascular fitness. Normal resting heart rate for adults ranges from 60 to 100; conditioned athletes will be on the low end of this range, and some athletes will have a resting heart rate even lower than 60. Those with a lower resting heart rate will likely see less of a drop in heart rate after a relaxation session.

Preparing for a Relaxation Session

Record Relaxation Instructions. When initially learning how to relax, some find it helpful to record the directions for relaxation. The recording can be played to lead you through a relaxation session. You can use the directions for deep breathing in **Exercise 6.1: Deep Breathing to Release Tension and Relax** or you can find other directions online (e.g., for progressive muscle relaxation, where you first intentionally tense then relax specific muscle groups throughout the body in order to learn to recognize the feelings of tension and then to control the tension by replacing it with relaxation). Using a recorder, read the directions in a calm voice.

Watch/Timer. You will need a timer to record your pulse/heart rate for 30 seconds both before and after the relaxation session.

Relaxation Questionnaire. Have a copy of the pre- and the post-questionnaires nearby (exercise sheets 6.2a and 6.2b), along with a pen or pencil.

Setting. Some find it helpful to be in a quiet setting in a dimly lit room, especially when first learning how to relax.

You can use both this exercise sheet and exercise sheet 6.2b in conjunction with **Exercise 6.2: Tracking Your Relaxation**.

Exercise sheet 6.2a

Name: _____   **Date:** _____

PRE-RELAXATION QUESTIONNAIRE

Please indicate the extent to which you agree or disagree with each item. There are no right or wrong answers. Please answer how you actually feel right now.

Pre-Relaxation Session	Strongly Disagree	Disagree	Neither Agree nor Disagree	Agree	Strongly Agree	Scoring[a]
1. I feel calm.	1	2	3	4	5	Rating =
2. I am relaxed.	1	2	3	4	5	Rating =
3. I am anxious.	1	2	3	4	5	(6 - Rating) =
4. I feel nervous.	1	2	3	4	5	(6 - Rating) =
5. I feel tension in some muscles.	1	2	3	4	5	(6 - Rating) =
6. I feel rested or refreshed.	1	2	3	4	5	Rating =
7. I feel warm.	1	2	3	4	5	Rating =
8. My muscles are relaxed.	1	2	3	4	5	Rating =
How much caffeine have you had today?[b] #____ ounces of _____ (e.g., 12 ounces of coffee)						TOTAL =

[a] To compute an overall Total Relaxation Questionnaire score, first subtract your ratings for item 3, item 4, and item 5 from 6, then add these numbers with the ratings for items 1, 2, 6, 7, and 8.
[b] The questionnaire inquires about caffeine intake because caffeine can cause your heart rate to be elevated.

HEART RATE (PULSE RATE)

Before you begin the relaxation session, take your heart rate. Count your heart beats for 30 seconds, then multiply by 2 to determine the rate per minute. Record this number below.

PRE-Session Heart Rate: _____
(Beats per Minute)

You can use both this exercise sheet and exercise sheet 6.2a in conjunction with **Exercise 6.2: Tracking Your Relaxation**.

Exercise sheet 6.2b

POST-RELAXATION QUESTIONNAIRE

After the relaxation session is completed, again take your heart rate and record it below.

POST-Session Heart Rate: _____
(Beats per Minute)

What % of the time were you fully attending to relaxing (rather than distracting thoughts)?
_____% of the time I was fully focused on relaxing.

Now complete the POST-Session Questionnaire. Please indicate the extent to which you agree or disagree with each item. There are no right or wrong answers. Please answer how you actually feel right now

Post-Relaxation Session	Strongly Disagree	Disagree	Neither Agree nor Disagree	Agree	Strongly Agree	Scoring[a]
1. I feel calm.	1	2	3	4	5	Rating =
2. I am relaxed.	1	2	3	4	5	Rating =
3. I am anxious.	1	2	3	4	5	(6 - Rating) =
4. I feel nervous.	1	2	3	4	5	(6 - Rating) =
5. I feel tension in some muscles.	1	2	3	4	5	(6 - Rating) =
6. I feel rested or refreshed.	1	2	3	4	5	Rating =
7. I feel warm.	1	2	3	4	5	Rating =
8. My muscles are relaxed.	1	2	3	4	5	Rating =
How much caffeine have you had today?[b] #____ ounces of _____ (e.g., 12 ounces of coffee)						TOTAL =

[a] To compute an overall Total Relaxation Questionnaire score, first subtract your ratings for item 3, item 4, and item 5 from 6, then add these numbers with the ratings for items 1, 2, 6, 7, and 8.
[b] The questionnaire inquires about caffeine intake because caffeine can cause your heart rate to be elevated.

There are many mindfulness exercises readily available on the web. The techniques described here are quite basic but will enable you to begin to develop mindfulness skills.

Exercise 6.3: Mindfulness of Our Senses

This exercise will help you become more aware of each of your senses. Set a timer for 60 seconds for each sense. As you become better at mindfulness focusing, you may wish to extend the time for each sense to 90 seconds or 120 seconds. If you become distracted during this exercise, gently refocus your attention to the sense you are trying to target. Try to experience each sense with acceptance rather than evaluating what you experience as good or bad.

Begin this mindfulness exercise with three deep breaths as described in **Exercise 6.1: Deep Breathing to Release Tension and Relax**. Once you are relaxed, go through the exercise for each sense. This exercise can be modified to include only one or several of the senses.

Vision/Sight. Start your timer. Look straight ahead and focus on a single object. Study that object. Rather than using self-talk to label what you see, notice the characteristics that define what you see, such as color, shape, and texture. Now broaden your focus and see what is ahead of you, to your left, to your right, Turn your head as far as you can to see all that is in your environment. Again, rather than using self-talk to label what you see, notice the characteristics that define what you see, such as color, shape, and texture.

Tactile/Touch. Start your timer. Notice the different textures that surround you in your clothes, your chair, and decorations in the room and on the wall. Touch the different textures and attend to how they feel; note the difference in the texture of your clothes, your hair, the wall, and the ground. Try to fully focus on how things feel.

Olfactory/Smell. Start your timer. Close your eyes and notice the smells in your environment. Bring your wrist to your nose to smell the scent of your own skin. Do you smell the aroma of any food or spice? Do you smell a sweet fragrance? What other smells do you detect? Try to accept and appreciate any smell that you encounter.

Gustatory/Taste. Before you start this exercise, collect a few things that are safe to put into your mouth (e.g., gum, food, or drink). Start your timer. Introduce one item into your mouth. Notice the flavor – is it sweet, sour, salty, or something else? Try to focus fully on the taste and flavor of what is in your mouth.

Auditory/Hearing. Start your timer. Use a soft or muted signal for the end of the 60 seconds. Close your eyes. Listen carefully for the different sounds you can hear. Try to distinguish separate sounds. Listen for the sound of your own breathing. What other sounds do you hear around you?

Exercise 6.3a: Mindfully Experience a Raisin

For this exercise you will mindfully experience a raisin. You will need several raisins – even if you do not like them. However, if you are allergic to raisins, you should do this exercise with another readily available food with an interesting texture.

Vision/Sight. Start your timer. Look at the raisin. Notice the color of the raisin and variations in color. Notice the wrinkles on the raisin, the tiny mark on the raisin where a stem once attached the grape to the bunch of grapes. Turn the raisin over in your hand so that you view all parts of the raisin.

Tactile/Touch. Start your timer. Notice the texture of the raisin. Note that it is smooth in some parts and wrinkled in others. Run your finger over the wrinkles and note how this feels. Notice how the raisin responds when you apply gentle pressure. Now apply more pressure until the raisin has a smoother surface. Did the raisin burst open? If so, feel the difference in the texture on the inside and outside of the raisin.

Olfactory/Smell. Start your timer. Close your eyes and notice how the raisin smells. Can you distinguish the fragrances of the inside of the raisin and the outside of the raisin? Are you able to focus on only the scent of the raisin?

Gustatory/Taste. Start your timer. Now bite the raisin in half. Hold the half raisin in your mouth. Notice the taste. Let the raisin rest on your tongue so that you are aware of the full flavor of the raisin.

Auditory/Hearing. Start your timer. Very slowly chew the first half of the raisin; listen to the sound of your mouth and tongue moving as you chew. Slowly swallow the half raisin and note the sound you make as you swallow. Now slowly chew the second half of the raisin and again listen to the sound of your chewing and slowly swallowing the raisin.

After completing this exercise, you will have experienced a raisin with all of your senses. Think about other common activities you engage in that you could practice more mindfully, with more of your senses. Note also that if you are fully focused on the raisin (100% of your attention), you cannot also be focused on worries or concerns. Thus, mindfulness can provide a brief break from issues that are distracting you or causing you to worry. Frequently, individuals feel more refreshed and ready to deal with problems after a mindfulness break.

Exercise 6.4: Other Brief Mindfulness Exercises

Make the Old New Again

Human nature causes us to habituate to things we encounter regularly such as the rooms in our homes, our office, our family, and our friends. Habituation refers to the fact that humans decrease their response (both perceptual and emotional) to things they are repeatedly exposed to. Habituation has benefits in that we do not have to relearn a room or a person each time we encounter them. However, habituation also means we lose the appreciation we once had with things that are now familiar. This exercise will help you regain the pleasure you may have lost to habituation.

Directions. Choose something that is very familiar to you. It can be something simple such as the pen you regularly write with, a key piece of equipment from your sport, or your cell phone; or it may be something more complex such as a photo of your team or loved one, or your locker room or playing field. Look at the object with a fresh perspective and try to notice details you had not noticed before or details that you had forgotten.

Attentive Listening

It is not uncommon for our minds to wander when we are engaged in conversation and should be fully attending to what others are saying. Sometimes we may be distracted; other times we are responding in our minds by evaluating what is being said, thinking of rebuttals or explanations, or other comments; and sometimes we might even interrupt the other person. Regardless of what is going on in our mind, we are not giving our full attention to the speaker. Next time your coach or teammate is speaking to you, try to listen with your complete attention. Try to fully understand what is being said before attempting to evaluate or respond. Active listening generally is a good communication skill and has been summarized as "seek first to understand." It is only after actively and fully listening to the speaker and delaying judgment or criticism that we can ensure complete understanding. (BTW, if you have fully attended and still do not understand what is being said, this is a good time to ask your coach or teammate for more information. Most people are happy to provide a better explanation when they know you have been listening attentively.)

Automaticity and Practice

7

Yes, you do need to practice. Elite athletes recognize the importance of practice and realize that, because opportunities to practice are limited, they need to take advantage of every practice session by focusing on developing specific skills and working hard – even when they do not feel like it. Feedback from coaches during practice is important in ensuring proper technique and mechanics. Successful athletes appreciate and look forward to practice and seek demanding practices that present a challenge. Do you appreciate practice, especially demanding practices? If you want to succeed at the highest levels you should. To answer the question, "How do I get maximum benefit from my practice?" requires a bit of background.

Mental Skills: Automaticity

When learning a motor skill, we progress through three stages: verbal, procedural, and autonomous. In the first, early stage of learning we "talk" ourselves through the skill; it requires our full attention; and we often work from instructions or examples. Think of trying to teach one of the basic skills in your sport – you start by verbally telling the individual what to do, perhaps while demonstrating the skill. The individual learning the skill likely talks him/herself through the execution of the skill. For example, "assume the ready stance (balanced with knees shoulder width apart), grip the golf club lightly in your hand, etc." As we practice a skill, the repetition moves us to the procedural stage where we go from knowing "what to do" to knowing "how to do it." For example, we now take our stance, grip the club, and get ready to swing without any verbalization or talking to ourselves. Performance becomes more fluid and error free and the verbalization drops out. With continued and **consistent** practice, the skill becomes automated and we do not have to think about performance. In fact, at the autonomous stage thinking about how to execute interferes with performance. To illustrate this, just ask a golfer if he exhales or inhales during his backswing. As the golfer thinks about this, it disrupts the automaticity of his smooth swing and interferes with performance. This is why many coaches tell their athletes, "Don't think about it. Just do it." Thinking about performing an automated skill interferes with automaticity.

There are a number of benefits of practicing to and beyond the point of automating component skills that are key to effective performance.

An automated skill:

1. Is performed **more efficiently**; it requires less energy and effort.
2. Is performed **more accurately** (provided practice has been accurate execution of the skill).
3. Is performed **faster**.
4. No longer requires attentional resources; that is, automated skills **require little thought or attention** and free up our attentional space so we can focus on other dynamic components of the performance situation.
5. Is **less susceptible to the effects of stress and fatigue**.
6. Is **better retained over long periods of time** than skills that require our active attention to perform.
7. Once initiated, **runs to completion** unless a conscious effort is made to stop the performance.
8. **Can occur without intentionally thinking about it** in the presence of the right stimulus. For example, if a defensive player in volleyball has automated the skill of digging the ball as it is spiked over the net, when the ball comes over the net, she will dig the ball without even thinking about it.

Most performance in a competitive situation is composed of a combination of cognitively controlled and automatically processed components. Consistency is the key to automating skills. Skills or skill components that are consistent can be automatized. The extent of improvement in performance by automating skills is directly related to the extent of consistency with which the skill/skill component is practiced. By automating the component skills that can be automated, it frees up cognitive space for analyzing the situation and making decisions. Think about a young child who has just learned to dribble a basketball. The child is watching his/her hand as they dribble, demonstrating that this skill is still being controlled by thought and is taking up most of the attentional space in the child's mind. Now, think about basketball player Steph Curry as he dribbles the ball down the court. The skill of dribbling the ball is so automated that it requires no thought and Steph can use all of his attentional space to read the court, see opponents' positions, and decide whether to shoot or pass to a teammate.

Skills at the automated level are less susceptible to the effects of stress and fatigue. Hence, we want to practice skills such as accurate strokes until our skills (e.g., driving, pitching, chipping, putting, etc.) are automated to the point that an accurate swing is the response we perform even under stressful conditions.

Familiar examples of automaticity in everyday life are illustrated by driving a car, a skill that is automated for many adults in the United States. Have you ever thought you needed to stop by the store on the way home from practice but, once you are in the car, you drove straight home – like you have done hundreds of times before? Have you ever had an engaging conversation on your cell phone as you drive home only to arrive at your home and not remember driving home? In both of these examples, the behavior of driving home is automated and did not rely on active attention. Automaticity also is why you may be able to drive somewhat impaired by alcohol or while texting (both of which are risky and very dangerous). Automaticity will work for you – unless something that requires your attention occurs such as a traffic light turning yellow, a curve in the road, another motorist swerving, or a child running out into the street. If any of these (or other situations) occur, your automated skill will most likely result in an accident that could prove very harmful for you or another.

Performance psychologists realize the importance of automating task components. Practice schedules should be structured to capitalize on the benefits of automaticity to optimize training and, ultimately, competitive performance. To capitalize on automaticity, we need to identify tasks and task components that can and cannot be automatized. Generally tasks or task components that are performed consistently each time the skill is executed can be automated. Examples include free throws, serving, swinging a golf club, hitting, etc. Controlled thought processes are required for the performance of novel tasks (such as a new play or a new skill) and tasks that are varied each time they are performed such that they require thought and attention (such as a quarterback searching for an open receiver). Thought-controlled tasks are difficult to perform concurrently with other tasks that are not automated. For example, you can walk and chew gum at the same time because both tasks are automated, but it is difficult to do multiplication tasks at the same time you are attentively listening to a conversation. (**Note:** Multi-tasking while completing any task that requires thought or decision making will result in lower performance on that task.)

Mental Skills: Perfect Practice Makes Perfect

What are the implications of the three stages of learning for practice? The most important implication is that you will play like you practice – so practice like you want to compete. That is, **consistently** perform each skill as perfectly as you can execute it. Play with the level of effort you need to demonstrate in competition. Have a positive attitude in practice. All of these, performance, effort, and attitude, will become automated. If you slack off in practice, you will automate slack performance. If you allow yourself to respond negatively to poor performance in practice, you will respond negatively in competition. It is perfect practice that leads to perfect (or near perfect) performance.

Novice athletes or athletes learning a new skill start out in the verbal stage and talk themselves through each skill or play. Practice and repetition will move the novice athlete to the procedural stage where s/he can perform without the "talk." Novice athletes or athletes learning a new skill or a new play need to **consistently** practice enough reps until each skill is automated. In fact, overlearning (practice beyond the point of successful performance) is key to automating skills.

Skilled athletes should practice under a variety of conditions (e.g., golfers should practice on the course, not just off the flat practice area; basketball players should shoot at a variety of goals; swimmers should swim in a variety of pools). Keeping skill performance **consistent** under varying practice conditions builds automaticity for the consistent skill regardless of where it is performed. For example, unless you are a golfer for whom all of his/her game shots land on the fairway or green, practice from a variety of lies; hit from the rough;

hit different clubs in various order. This increases the generalizability of your automated stroke to different lies and course conditions. Adapting to changing conditions becomes automated. Another example of the importance of varied practice is seen in shooting free throws in basketball. Generally, who are the best free throw shooters? Guards, who shoot field goals from around the top of the key, typically are the best free-throw shooters. The post players, who primarily shoot field goals in the lane near the basket, typically are not as proficient at free throws. Although most coaches have players practice free throws from the free throw line (consistent practice conditions), there is some research evidence that shooting from a variety of positions around the free throw line also will lead to increased free throw proficiency. Shooting 15 feet from the basket over many reps from a variety of locations can help automate the 15-foot shot whether it is from the free throw line or some other spot around the top of the key.

Automaticity explains why it is hard to break bad habits – the bad habit has been repeated until it became the dominant, automated response. Automaticity also is why we often see an initial drop in performance when changing how we perform a skill – we are fighting the old but strong automated way of performing the skill while moving back to the verbal or procedural stage to learn the new, corrected performance of the skill. Practice/repetition until the new performance is automated is the way to make the new, corrected skill the dominant response that will be given in stressful competitive situations. Using performance cues (as described in Chapter 2) will help ensure the correct response while building automaticity and, once the skill is automated, will serve as a cue to your mind to call up the now automated motor program for the skill.

Key Concepts in Automaticity and Practice

Automate important component skills for your sport. Skills that are automated are performed more efficiently and accurately, and are more resistant to the effects of stress and fatigue. Thus, automating important skills is especially important for high demand performance situations like key competitions, play offs, or the Olympics.

Identify consistent component skills to be automated. Consistent task components must be identified and trained to levels of automaticity to minimize the cognitive demands of performance. The greater the number of task components that are automated, the lower the mental workload and the more the attentional space that will be free for analyzing the situation and decision making.

Vary practice conditions. Practicing under a variety of conditions automates the ability to adapt to different conditions. Vary the conditions of practice (e.g., the field, the goal, the piece of equipment, etc.); however, the skilled response itself should be practiced consistently (e.g., technique and form for shooting, turns in swimming, serve routine, etc.).

Practice like you want to play. Guidelines to make your practice more effective are:

1. Plan what you want to accomplish at each practice session.
2. Keep a record of your practice performance (e.g., in golf: fairways hit, greens in regulation, etc.). Supplement these stats with comments about what went well and what needs more work.

3. Use your stats to set goals for future practice sessions.
4. Practice like you play. For example, putt with one ball and putt it in. Chip and putt to different targets. Use your shot routine during practice.
5. Work with your coach to ensure that you are practicing proper technique and execution. Work on the weak part of your game and work to maintain your strengths.

Remember, it is not simply "practice that makes perfect," but "*perfect* practice that makes perfect."

Routines 8

Routines are strongly recommended for closed skills. Closed skills are skills that are performed in a predictable environment where the response can be planned and executed without interference from an opponent and, even if there is a time limit, the skill is self-paced. Closed skills include shooting in archery, basketball free throws, serving in several sports, penalty kicks in soccer, gymnastics, diving, football kickoffs and field goals, and golf. Open skills are performed in a dynamic environment that is not controlled by the athlete. Open skills require responding to the specific but changing characteristics of the immediate situation. Open skills include basketball field goal shooting, dribbling in soccer, hitting and serve receive in volleyball, and passing and running in football. Some skills contain both open and closed skill components. To the extent that closed skills are involved, a routine will increase consistency and effectiveness in performance. Using a routine each time you execute a closed skill helps to build automaticity – so, be sure you are properly executing your skill (check with your skills coach).

A routine helps you concentrate and block out distractions; it increases your trust in your performance, whether, for example, serving in tennis or volleyball, shooting free throws, hitting a golf ball, or pitching a baseball or softball. A good routine draws on two different parts of your mind: "The Thinker" and "The Doer." The Thinker is the part of the mind that analyzes the situation, controls self-talk, and sets goals for your performance. The Doer controls the automatic performance that has been built in your muscle memory from repetition in practice and play. Examples of routines for several sports are given later in this chapter. This chapter addresses the pre-performance routine. For some sports, a post-performance routine also may be applicable.

Mental Skills: Using a Performance Routine

A pre-performance routine consists of two phases. Phase I relies on The Thinker; Phase II on the Doer. The first step in Phase I is to relax using a relaxation technique you feel comfortable with (e.g., one-breath relaxation or cue-controlled relaxation – see Chapter 6).

Being relaxed sends a message to your mind that you are calm and in control, which in turn increases confidence. Next you should analyze the situation. Attend to relevant information that helps you determine the best way to execute your skill (e.g., serve, stroke, shot, or pitch). Make a decision on the execution characteristics and the objective for the skill (e.g., the target, the target line, the desired flight path, speed, and the motion you will execute to get the ball to the target). The final (optional) component of Phase I is to use imagery to rehearse perfect execution of your skill. Imagery will call up the muscle memory for the performance you wish to execute. If you have practiced relaxation and imagery, Phase I of the pre-performance routine can take as little as 5 to 10 seconds.

Now move to Phase II of the pre-performance routine. Some athletes use relaxation again as they move from Phase I into Phase II. If you are still loose and comfortable, additional relaxation is not needed. If you feel a little anxious or tight, then repeat the relaxation prior to the performance thought (see immediately below) in Phase II.

You now know your performance objective and desired execution from Phase I. Phase II relies on The Doer mind and begins when you are prepared to execute the skill. It is helpful for many athletes to use a performance thought or performance cue at the beginning of Phase II to trigger the performance. A performance thought is a single word or a short phrase that captures the essence of your desired performance. Serve thoughts might be phrases such as "Palm to target" when serving in volleyball or, for pitching a baseball, "Let the grip do the work." Use the performance cue consistently as part of your pre-performance routine.

In Phase II, it is critical that you trust the automaticity you have developed for your skill over many hours of practice. You have practiced many repetitions through actual practice, imagery, and competition so that the performance should be strong in your muscle memory. In Phase II, use your performance thought then execute. Just do it. At this point you do **not** want to think about your performance. Thinking about the performance disrupts the automatic performance driven by the muscle memory. Questioning creates doubt, decreases confidence, and causes hesitation in the performance. Hence the adage that if you want to mess up your opponent's performance just ask him if he inhales or exhales on the backswing. Simply thinking about when one breathes is enough to disrupt the automatic muscle memory and throw the swing out of kilter.

To sum up Phase II, use your performance thought, trust your decisions from Phase 1, and then execute. Using a routine each time you execute your skill helps to ensure consistency in your focus and in your execution.

Practice

Closed skills are unique because the action is stopped and you are in control. Essentially, the skill should be executed the same way every time it occurs (especially when you use your mental skills to block out the context; i.e., the game situation and other distractions). The more you practice your skill, the stronger the muscle memory for the correct form, the more automatic the skill will become, and the better your execution will be in competition. For example, some basketball coaches believe you should practice free throws until you are able to shoot them with your eyes closed. Practice should include lots of time on the court, field, etc., as well as mental rehearsal. Setting goals for your skill and tracking your performance will help you monitor your performance and motivate you to keep improving.

Superstitions

Superstitions develop when some action is followed by a positive outcome even though there is no relationship between the behavior and the outcome. Athletes (and fans – e.g., rally caps) that adopt superstitious behaviors engage in rituals that they believe positively impact their performance in competition – despite there being no relationship between the two. For example, Pistol Pete Maravich, arguably the best shooter in NBA history, wore the same pair of socks every game and never washed the socks during the season. Michael Jordan wore his University of North Carolina shorts under his Chicago Bulls uniform in every game during his six NBA championships career with the Bulls. Swedish tennis champion Bjorn Borg grew a beard before every one of his five straight Wimbledon titles. A number of NFL and NHL players and other athletes have adopted the beard superstition. Serena Williams, another tennis great, engages in a number of superstitious rituals behaviors including tying her shoelaces a specific way and wearing the same socks throughout a tournament. As part of her serve routine, she bounces the ball five times before her first serve and twice before her second serve.

Are superstitions helpful or harmful? To the extent that superstitious behavior boosts confidence, it can be helpful. However, importantly, remember that the essence of mental toughness is feeling that you are in control. You should avoid superstitions that rely on events that are out of your control (e.g., what someone else does, the weather, a specific article of clothing that could be forgotten or lost). If your superstition is under your control (e.g., growing a beard, bouncing the ball three times, etc.) and it gives you a sense of confidence, it is not a problem. If, however, your superstition is dependent on outside factors or interferes with your or your teammates' performance, you are setting yourself up for disappointment.

Key Concepts in Routines

Routines are very helpful for closed skills. A routine helps you concentrate and block out distractions, and increases trust in your performance. A routine helps to build automaticity and ensure consistency in performance. Complex skills will be performed more effectively if a routine is used to practice until the component skills are automated. Using the routine in competition will help to ensure successful performance under stressful conditions.

A good routine draws on the two different parts of your mind: "The Thinker" and "The Doer." The Thinker is the part of the mind that analyzes the situation, controls self-talk, and sets goals for performance. The Doer controls the automatic performance that is built in your muscle memory from repetition in practice and play.

Phase I of the Routine: The Thinker. In Phase I, relax, analyze the situation, and make decisions. Commit to those decisions.

Phase II of the Routine: The Doer. In Phase II, trust your execution of the skill and rely on automaticity. Use a performance cue to trigger the motor memory for the skill, then "just do it" without thinking about the performance.

Use your routine in practice and in competition. Using the same routine every time you execute the skill (in practice and in games) helps to automate the skill (with all of the benefits of automaticity – more efficient, more resistant to stress, more resistant to fatigue) and helps to ensure consistency in performance. Use your routine in your imagery when you visualize yourself performing the skill.

Examples of Routines for Different Sports

The following are examples of routines for closed skills from several different sports. The basic components of each routine in Phase I and Phase II are the same even though each routine is adapted for the specific sport and the specific skill. For some closed skills (e.g., golf swing), a Phase III: Post-Execution Routine may be useful.

Example 8.1: Golf Swing Routine

A shot routine helps you concentrate and block out distractions, and increases your trust in your swing. A good shot routine draws on the two different parts of your mind: "The Thinker" and "The Doer." The Thinker is the part of the mind that analyzes the situation, controls self-talk, and sets goals for your shot. The Doer controls the automatic performance that is built in your muscle memory from repetition in practice and play. The routine below is used by a number of golfers.

Phase I: The Thinker

- Relax using a relaxation technique you feel comfortable with (e.g., one-breath relaxation or cue-controlled relaxation). Being relaxed sends a message to your mind that you are calm and in control, which in turn increases confidence.
- Analyze the situation. Attend to relevant information such as lie, distance, and obstacles. Make a decision on shot selection and the objective for the shot (i.e., the target, the target line, the desired flight path, club selection, and the swing you will execute to get the ball to the target).
- Use a practice swing and/or imagery to rehearse perfect execution of your shot. Imagery or a practice swing will call up the muscle memory for the shot you wish to execute.

If you have practiced relaxation and imagery, Phase I of the Pre-Shot Routine can take as little as 10 to 30 seconds.

Phase II: The Doer

You know your shot objective and desired execution from Phase I. Some golfers use relaxation again as they move from Phase I into Phase II. If you are still loose and comfortable, additional relaxation is not needed. If you feel a little anxious or tight, then repeat the relaxation at this point. Phase II begins when you are prepared to hit the ball.

- Trust your swing and trust your decisions from Phase I.
- Use your swing thought.
- Execute.

Using a swing thought or performance cue in Phase II helps to trigger the motor memory for your swing. A swing thought is a single word or a short phrase that captures the essence of your desired swing. Swing thoughts might be phrases such as "smooth," "easy does it," or "inside out." Your swing thought likely will change depending on whether it is your drive, approach shot, or putt. Use a swing thought consistently as part of your pre-shot routine.

Phase III: The Post-Shot Routine

After you have hit the ball, move into your post-shot routine. Phase III of the Shot Routine again involves using the Thinker part of your mind to observe the outcome of the swing. You either hit the shot just as you planned or miss hit the shot to varying degrees. If you executed well, great! Now, store that shot in motor memory by mentally rehearsing it and perhaps repeating the swing. This will reinforce muscle memory for the well-executed swing.

The post-shot routine for a missed shot involves two steps. First, correct the error(s). Use positive imagery to see and feel yourself executing the perfect swing. Likewise, you can take a practice swing to correct the stroke. Either of these actions will help replace the poor performance with proper execution in muscle memory. Second, let go of the error. Forget about it. Flush it from your mind. It is now history. You cannot (legally) go back in time and replay the shot. You have done what you can to correct the shot in your motor memory. Now, move on to your next shot. The power is in the present. Your opportunity to positively impact your score now lies with your current shot and fully focusing to make the most of this situation.

Example 8.2: Volleyball Serve Routine

This serve routine was developed for intercollegiate volleyball players. A routine helps you control the serve, concentrate, and block out distractions; a routine increases your trust in your serve. When serving, use two parts of your mind: the "Thinker" and the "Doer."

1. The Thinker is the part of the mind that analyzes the situation, controls self-talk, and sets goals for your serve.
2. The Doer controls the automatic performance that is built in your muscle memory from repetition in practice and play. The Doer relies on motor memory and automatic performance.

Phase I: Thinker

* Relax – take a deep breath; relax; be calm and in control.
* Select the target zone.
* Commit - set a goal for the serve including pace/speed, trajectory, and placement.
* Imagery – see and feel the serve.

Phase II: The Doer

* Trust your serve (you have practiced so many repetitions (practice and imagery) that serving successfully should be very strong in your muscle memory).
* Use your serve thought "Straight Line" or "Palm to Target" to trigger your serve. You may also use a different serve trigger that works you (e.g., "Strong and Straight"), but your serve trigger should be consistent (i.e., use the same trigger every time you serve).
* Execute – just do it; serve the ball. Trust your serve; do not think about it; rely on your automatic muscle memory to "just do it." Thinking about the serve disrupts the automatic performance; questioning creates doubt, decreases confidence, and slows reaction time. After you have served the ball, get ready for action.

Phase III: The Post-Serve Routine

When the ball is dead, reflect on the outcome of your serve.

* For a good serve – reinforce the successful serve through imagery (repeat the serve in your imagery); feel good about your serve.
* For a missed serve – use positive imagery to correct errors and to rehearse proper serving. Then, let go of the error and forget about it.
* Move on – focus on the "3 Ps", the Positive Present Performance; what you need to do right now to make your team successful (whether it is execute another serve or defense).

After the competition is over, you can use imagery to review the match, to reinforce good performance, and to correct errors.

Example 8.3: Basketball Free Throw Routine

With a free throw, there is little decision making as the goal is always the same – make the shot. The basket is the same height and distance from the line in every situation. If you use mental skills to block out distractions and context, the success of the free throw depends on technique/mechanics. Many basketball coaches use the acronym "BEEF" to sum up good technique for free throw shooting. Get your shot coach to check your mechanics/technique.

B – **Balance:** feet shoulder width apart, knees flexed.

E – **Elbows in:** in line with the basket; not sticking out from your sides.

E – **Eyes on the target:** aim; use your eye-hand coordination to evoke motor memory for the shot.

F – **Follow through:** your arm should extend and your hand should "follow" the ball all the way through the basket (like stealing a cookie from a cookie jar on a high self).

Develop a routine for your shot and follow it every time you shoot a free throw, whether it is in practice or in a game. The routine should be your own, but should probably include the following:

Phase I: The Thinker

- Step to the line, place feet in a balanced position.
- Relax – use the cue word from your relaxation techniques or take between one and three deep, slow breaths.
- Use a narrow external focus of attention; block out everything else except for the goal.
- Use mental rehearsal to "practice" the shot in your mind; focus on the using the proper form (BEEF) and seeing the ball go through the net in your imagery.

Phase II: The Doer

- Execute – shoot the free throw.

Some players will add three dribbles before the shot or some other extra component to their routine. This is fine as long as it positively contributes to the routine (i.e., does not distract from technique or focus). The important thing is to develop a routine and use it every time you shoot a free throw.

Example 8.4: Baseball Pitching Routine

Using the same routine every time you pitch (in practice and in games) helps to automate your pitching (with all of the benefits of automaticity – more efficient, more resistant to stress, more resistant to fatigue) and helps to ensure consistency in your pitching. Use your routine in your imagery when you visualize yourself pitching. I developed this routine with a major league pitcher.

Phase I: The Thinker

- Receive ball from catcher as a signal to focus. Use self-talk: "Be Aggressive. Be Down in the Zone."
- Step to the back of the mound.
- Straddle the rubber.
- Focus on a specific spot in the distance.
- Take a deep slow breath to relax.
- Decide on pitch; commit 100% to the pitch; tell catcher what pitch.

Phase II: The Doer

- Step back on the rubber.
- Use performance cue/affirmation statement specific to the pitch.
- Trust the pitch decision.
- Just throw it.

Develop Your Own Routine – Example with Punting in Football

You may be able to adapt one of the routines described above for a closed skill in your sport. Work with your coach to identify the proper technique and mechanics for the skill and the key decisions that need to be made before executing the skill. If, for example, you are the punter on a football team, you need to consider the objective for the punt, the placement of the ball on the field, the distance, hang time, direction, and any environmental factors such as wind or rain. A routine for punting might include the following steps.

Phase I: Thinker

- Relax – take a deep breath; relax; be calm and in control.
- Analyze the situation; consider the relevant factors.
- Commit – set the goal for the kick including pace/speed, trajectory, and placement.
- Imagery – see and feel the kick.

Phase II: The Doer

- Trust your kick and trust your decisions from Phase I.
- If you have a performance cue, use it to trigger muscle memory and automaticity.
- Execute – catch the snap, drop the ball, and kick the ball. Do not think about execution, just do it.

Using your routine in practice will help to automate the component skills (i.e., holding the ball, stepping forward, dropping the ball, and contact). Punting is a complex skill that will be performed more effectively if a routine is used to practice until the component skills are automated. Using the routine in competition will help to ensure successful punts under stressful conditions.

Part III

Team Skills and Special Situations

Part III

Team Skills and Special
Situations

Role Clarity for Team Sports

9

The contribution of the individual athlete is central to the success of any team. Each athlete must have a thorough understanding of his/her responsibilities on the team and the behavior needed to fulfill those responsibilities. A team member who misunderstands his/her team roles likely is a hindrance to team effectiveness and to the accomplishment of team objectives. When team member roles are critical, interdependent, highly differentiated and non-redundant, the failure to perform role assignments by a single team member may result in ineffectiveness for the entire team. Role clarity is an important prerequisite to team effectiveness, as the actions of a single team member may have a dramatic impact on total team performance.

Role ambiguity refers to uncertainty and a lack of role clarity regarding one's role in the performance setting. There is a negative relationship between role ambiguity and performance, and between role ambiguity and other performance-related variables such as satisfaction and commitment.

Effective communication between the coach and each athlete regarding his/her role responsibilities is critical to role clarity and, subsequently, to the success of the team. Roles within a team setting must develop and change over time to meet the changing demands of the competitive situation. Failure to recognize and communicate the need for role change can result in stagnation and failure for both the individual athlete and the team. At times, the stress of a long season can inhibit a coach's effectiveness in communicating with his/her athletes. In addition to the unstructured role communication that typically occurs in team situations, formal role clarity programs can be effective in influencing athletes' understanding of their roles on the team.

This chapter presents a structured process for improving coach–athlete role communication and for increasing role clarity for each athlete on the team. I have successfully used this process for intercollegiate basketball, volleyball, and football teams. The process is proactive and allows flexibility and preparedness in meeting the role demands placed on team members. It is likely that, with minor adaptations, the process could be used to increase role clarity in a number of team sports.

The primary objective of the role process is to increase role clarity and to concomitantly reduce role ambiguity. The role process intervention focuses on reducing task ambiguity. Task ambiguity can assume three specific forms: ambiguity about the scope of responsibilities (i.e., what is required), ambiguity about the behaviors required to accomplish those responsibilities, and ambiguity about whose expectations are to be met. The scope of responsibilities is clearly defined by objectively identifying the specific roles an athlete is to fill.

When this process was implemented for the teams I worked with, the specific behaviors required to accomplish each role were delineated in the definition of the role, in a meeting with the coach, and on the practice floor. These intercollegiate teams, like many at this level of play, were run in a fairly autocratic manner where the coach determined which athlete(s) should assume each role responsibility. The roles process requires a substantial amount of time from the head coach and several hours from the individual who tallies the data from the Role Grids and prepares the individual feedback sheets (this can be the head coach, an assistant coach, or a graduate assistant). However, the teams I have worked with found the role process to be well worth the investment of time in terms of increased athlete role understanding and role acceptance following the implementation of the process. Given the amount of time involved, one might be inclined to limit athlete participation in the roles process to only those athletes likely to get substantial playing time. A coach who values athlete development and maintaining commitment from all team members should implement the roles process for all athletes on the team. For example, the role process was useful in helping a red-shirted athlete recognize that he was an important part of the team and still had responsibilities on the team despite the fact that he would not be playing in competition.

A Structured Process for Increasing Role Clarity in Team Sports

Developing the Roles List. For the role clarity process to work effectively, it is necessary to identify and list the individual athlete roles that are needed for the team to be successful. These roles are then used to develop an instrument that is referred to as the "Roles Grid." Although there are certain roles that are essential for a given sport, the particular roles that belong on the list will differ from coach to coach within a sport depending upon that coach's game strategy and the athletes on the team. Across seasons, the particular roles may vary depending on what the coach is emphasizing in his/her system in a particular season.

The head coach serves as the subject matter expert to generate a comprehensive list of the roles required for effective team performance. The initial list of roles should be reviewed by others on the coaching staff and in a team session by the athletes to ensure that the list of critical roles is exhaustive and that the terminology used to describe the roles is clearly understood by the athletes. Modifications can be made to the list of roles based on the comments of the staff and athletes. During the team session, athletes should be encouraged to identify any role that is not clearly understood. Roles that might be misunderstood should be explicitly defined (e.g., that cheerleader is a positive, important role). It should be pointed out that a single athlete should have a limited number of roles; that no athlete could be expected to perform all of the roles; but, each athlete has specific roles for which s/he has a responsibility to fulfill. Example Roles Lists for basketball, volleyball, and football can be seen below. Be sure to note that even if you are in one of these sports, specific roles will likely vary depending on your team situation. Each of the terms used on the Roles List also could be included in the glossary section of the playbook studied by athletes on the team.

Basketball Roles	Volleyball Roles	Football – Inside Linebacker Roles
Scorer	Setter	On the Field Leader
Rebounder (Defense)	Hitter	Off the Field Leader
Defensive Stopper	Defensive Player	Signal Caller
Offensive Rebounder	Serve Receiver	Communicates Tendencies
Shot Blocker	Blocker	Communicates Adjustments
Floor Leader/Assist Leader	Server	Vocal/Emotional Leader
Emotional Floor Leader	Communicates on the Floor	Force Backer
3-Point Shooter	Emotional Leader	Scrape Backer
Intimidator/Physical Player	Practice Player	Zone Pass Coverage
Communicates on the Floor	Locker Room Leader	Match Pass Coverage
Spark Off the Bench	Competitive Leader	Man Pass Coverage
Cheerleader	Spark	Blitz/Pressure
Practice Player	Positive Influence	Practice/Scout Team Player
Off the Floor Leader		
Communicates to Coach Off the Floor		

The Role Grid. A table is created where the athletes on the team are the rows and the roles for the team are the columns. Each athlete and the head coach independently indicate from the list of roles the primary roles for each athlete on the team (i.e., three roles are indicated for each athlete by each teammate; up to five roles are indicated for each athlete by the coach and by each athlete as their own roles). The grids usually are completed in a team meeting to ensure all individuals complete a grid and to answer questions. In the meeting, the underlying rationale of the role clarification process and the procedure that will be followed is explained. That is, each athlete and the coach will independently complete a Role Grid to indicate the roles for the athletes on the team. The coach's assignment of roles identifies the role responsibilities for a specific player. The coach and player Role Grid responses will be tallied and individual role feedback will be discussed with each player in a one-on-one meeting with the coach.

Example of a Role Grid for Basketball

Directions

For each of your teammates, mark an "X" in the column for the three roles you most often see him/her perform.

For yourself, first circle your name and then mark an "X" in the column of the three to five roles you believe you most often perform.

Roles / Name	Scorer	Rebounder	Def Stopper	Off Rebounder	Shot Blocker	Floor Leader / Assist Leader	Emotional Floor Leader	3-Point Shooter	Intimidator Physical Player	Commutates on the Floor	Spark Off the Bench	Cheerleader	Practice Player	Off the Floor Leader	Comm to Coach Off Floor
Alex															
Bailey															
Cory															
Dominique															
Elm															
Finley															
Gray															
Harley															
Inman															
Jordan															
Kerry															
Lee															

Example of a Role Grid Completed by Dominique

Name	Scorer	Rebounder	Def Stopper	Off Rebounder	Shot Blocker	Floor Leader / Assist Leader	Emotional Floor Leader	3-Point Shooter	Intimidator Physical Player	Commutates on the Floor	Spark Off the Bench	Cheerleader	Practice Player	Off the Floor Leader	Comm to Coach Off Floor
Alex	x	x							x						
Bailey							x					x	x		
Cory			x	x	x										
Dominique	x	x	x				x								
Elm	x	x									x				
Finley												x	x	x	
Gray	x								x		x				
Harley	x					x			x						
Inman		x		x						x					
Jordan	x					x			x						
Kerry	x									x					x
Lee		x	x								x				

Aggregating Role Grid Data and Preparing Role Feedback Sheets. The grid data are tallied and an individual Team Role Perception Feedback Sheet is prepared for each athlete. The completed individual Feedback Sheets are presented to each athlete in an individual role clarification meeting between athlete and coach (that may be facilitated by a sport psychologist). The Feedback quadrants reveal: (1) roles recognized by the athlete, coach, and teammates; (2) roles the athlete and coach are aware of but are not recognized by teammates; (3) roles recognized by coach and teammates but not the athlete; and (4) roles only the coach recognizes; that is, roles that are not acknowledged by the athlete or other teammates.

A blank Role Grid can be used to tally the data from the coach and all team members. For each athlete, you will need to record: (1) the roles the coach assigned to the athlete; (2) the roles the athlete assigned to him/herself; and (3) the number of teammates who identified each role for that athlete. Prepare an individual Role Feedback Sheet for each athlete using this information. This information provides athletes with objective, relatively anonymous, multi-source feedback about how their role performance is perceived (or "not" perceived) by their teammates and provides the basis for the role discussion between the coach and each athlete.

Individual Role Feedback Meetings. The coach will then meet one-on-one with each team member to discuss his/her role responsibilities. During the individual sessions, athletes are encouraged to ask questions and to identify any role that was not clearly understood. The four cells on the Role Feedback Sheet provide information about how well the athlete understands his/her role and whether or not his/her teammates see him/her getting the job done for each role.

Cell Content of Role Perception Feedback Sheet

Cell 1 – Known to You/Known to Others: These roles are the roles the coach wants you to fulfill; you recognize them as your roles on the team, and your teammates see you getting them done. This is where you are doing a good job. However, if only a few teammates recognize this, you may need to focus more of your efforts on those roles.

Cell 2 – Unknown to You/Known to Others: These are roles that you do not identify as your primary roles, but your coach identifies them as your roles and your teammates see you getting them done. These are areas where you are making contributions to the team, but you do not recognize this. Give yourself credit for contributing on theses roles.

Cell 3: Known to You/Unknown to Others: You and your coach identify these as your roles, but your teammates do **not** see you getting them done. This cell represents roles you should be fulfilling (i.e., the coach and you know they are your roles), but others do **not** see you fulfilling these roles. You need to put more effort into these roles.

Cell 4: Unknown to You/Unknown to Others: These are roles the coach wants you to fulfill, but you do not own them as your roles and others do not see you getting these roles done. You need to put more effort into these roles.

Team Role Perception Feedback Sheet

You may use the blank Team Role Perception Feedback Sheet on the next page to prepare feedback for each of your athletes. Examples of Team Role Perception Feedback Sheets completed for Dominique, Alex, and Jordan may be found on pages 121 to 123.

Team Role Perception Feedback Sheet

Player: Date:

		YOU	
		KNOWN	**UNKNOWN**
OTHERS	**KNOWN**	**1** Other Players, Coach, & You	**2** Coach &/or Other Players
	UNKNOWN	**3** You & Coach	**4** Coach only

Note: Player's initial = player identified role for self, C= Coach identified role for player, # = number of players who identified that role for you

Team Role Perception Feedback Sheet for Dominique

Player: **DOMINIQUE**   Date: *January 16*

		YOU	
		KNOWN	**UNKNOWN**
OTHERS	**KNOWN**	*Scorer D, C, 10* *Defensive Stopper* *D, C, 10* **Cell 1:** Other Players, Coach, & You	 **Cell 2:** Coach &/or Other Players
	UNKNOWN	*Emotional Leader* *D, C, 2* *Rebounder D, C, 3* **Cell 3:** You & Coach	 **Cell 4:** Coach Only

Note: Player's initial = player identified role for self, C = Coach identified role for player, # = number of players who identified that role for you.

Team Role Perception Feedback Sheet for Alex

Player: ALEX   Date: January 16

		YOU	
		KNOWN	**UNKNOWN**

OTHERS	**KNOWN**	Rebounder A, C, 10
		Intimidator/
		Physical
		    Player A, C, 7
		Scorer A, MC, 6
		Defensive Stopper
		    A, C, 5
		
		Cell 1: Other Players, Coach, & You
			Cell 2: Coach &/or Other Players

	UNKNOWN	**Cell 3:** You & Coach	**Cell 4:** Coach Only

Note: Player's initial = player identified role for self, C= Coach identified role for player, # = number of players who identified that role for you.

Team Role Perceptions Feedback Sheet for Jordan

Player: JORDAN   Date: January 16

		YOU	
		KNOWN	UNKNOWN
OTHERS	KNOWN	Scorer J, C, 10 Floor Leader/ Asst. Ldr J, C, 10 3-Point Shooter J, C, 5* **Cell 1:** Other Players, Coach, & You	Off the Floor Leader C, 7* **Cell 2:** Coach &/or Other Players
	UNKNOWN	Emotional Leader J, C, 2* Communicates on the Floor J, C, 4* **Cell 3:** You & Coach	 **Cell 4:** Coach Only

Note: Player's initial = player identified role for self, C= Coach identified role for player, # = number of players who identified that role for you.

Let's examine the feedback sheets for three players Dominique, Alex, and Jordan, and what might be discussed in their individual meetings with Coach. All three players have a pretty good idea of their role responsibilities, but the data point out several areas for more role clarity.

Dominique. Dominique and Coach identified the same four roles: Scorer, Defensive Stopper, Rebounder, and Emotional Leader. This agreement indicates that Dominique knows what the coach wants done. Ten teammates identified Scorer and Defensive Stopper as roles they see Dominique accomplishing – indicating that Dominique is doing a good job with these roles. However, only three teammates identified Rebounder as a role they observe Dominique fulfilling. This suggests Dominique needs to step up on rebounding. Only two players identified Emotional Leader as a role they observed Dominique fulfilling. It is possible other players did not notice Dominique rebounding, but when teammates do not observe a leadership role, it is a good indication that role is not being fulfilled. Coach and Dominique need to recognize where Dominique is performing well, but they also need to discuss what Dominique needs to do to fulfill the roles of Rebounder and Emotional Leader.

Alex. Alex and Coach identified the same four roles: Rebounder, Intimidator/Physical Player, Scorer, and Defensive Stopper. Likewise, teammates observe Alex performing all four of these roles. Coach should reinforce the good job Alex is doing in fulfilling role responsibilities. If Coach would like, for example, more emphasis on Defensive Stopper and less emphasis on Intimidator, this could be discussed in the individual meeting with Alex.

Jordan. Clearly, Coach expects a lot from Jordan, who is a senior point-guard for the team. Jordan and Coach agree on four roles: Scorer, Floor Leader/Assist Leader, 3-Point Shooter, Emotional leader and Communicates on the Floor. Coach should recognize the good job Jordan is doing on Scorer, Floor Leader/Assist Leader, and 3-Point Shooter. Coach also wants Jordan to be an Off-the-Floor Leader and seven teammates observe Jordan in this role. Coach needs to let Jordan know that teammates look to him/her as an Off-the-Floor Leader, something Jordan is not aware of. Areas where Jordan needs to place more emphasis is on Communicates on the Floor and Emotional Leader. Coach may need to discuss if Jordan is capable of fulfilling this many important roles.

How Effective is the Role Process?

In my experience, most athletes perceive the feedback as accurate, providing them with new information, contributing to their understanding of team perceptions of their contribution, and useful to understanding their roles on the team. Following the individual role meetings, athletes typically have a high level of role understanding, acceptance, and commitment, suggesting that team members better understand what to do and are more willing to work hard to get it done.

Most athletes appreciate the one-on-one session with the coach. Although it requires substantial time from the coach, the structured process ensures the coach takes the time to communicate with each athlete. (One coach conducts the meetings with each athlete during down time while on the road for away games.) This role process can be a useful component of effective two-way communication between the coach and athlete.

Some of the teams I work with complete the roles process on three occasions across the season: once pre-season after practice had begun but before the first game; once mid-season; and once toward the end of the regular season. Having multiple meetings accommodated the dynamic nature of the athletes' roles. That is, as the prescribed roles for each athlete changed over the course of the season, it was reflected in the coach's role assignments and was discussed with the athlete in the roles meetings. The assistant coaches were consulted on roles throughout the season and received copies of the results of each of the three administrations of the roles process, but were not present at the roles meetings.

As a final step in the process, role signs can be made for each player identifying his/her role responsibilities and placed on lockers in the locker room. Role signs serve as a reminder of expectations for each athlete. If the role signs are on the outside of the locker, teammates know role responsibilities for every athlete on the team, which may lead to increased accountability toward role fulfillment. Goal setting and feedback in relation to role responsibilities helps to focus effort on role accomplishment. Feedback after each competition in terms of relevant statistics or other metrics helps the athlete track his/her role performance relative to his/her individual goals.

Playing Time. Some athletes do not get as much playing time as they would like and, consequently, are less satisfied with their role assignments. Even so, in my experience, the roles process increases their satisfaction with their roles on the team. An exercise that works for some sports is to have each player put his/her name on an index card and indicate how many minutes they would like to play in competition. The coach can collect the cards and add up the total number of minutes across all team members. This "desired total" can be compared to the actual total number of available minutes. For example, in basketball, five athletes play two 20-minute halves for a total of 200 available minutes. When the athletes are shown a total for desired minutes of 375 (for example) in comparison to the 200 total minutes actually available, they can see why not everyone can play as many minutes as they might like, and they have a better appreciation of why their playing time is limited. Hopefully, players will still want more minutes and will work hard in practice to earn those minutes.

Keys to Success of Roles Process. There are several reasons for the success of the role process. The roles process provides a structured format to assist the coach in communicating role information to the athletes. To complete the role process, the coach must make a conscious determination of which roles to assign to athletes. This forces the coach to have a definite plan for the roles for each athlete on the team. Certainly a coach should communicate role information on and off the court (I note that the coaches I have worked with certainly do). However, the dynamic environment of intercollegiate athletics and time constraints in practice often make it difficult for a coach to communicate fully and effectively with his/her athletes regarding their role responsibilities. The roles process is a technique that assists the coach in meeting this challenge by structuring an opportunity for one-on-one communication between the coach and the athlete. This improved communication increases the athlete's understanding of his/her roles. S/he has the opportunity to ask for clarification in a supportive climate that is more conducive to this sort of inquiry than a team practice might be. Athletes comment that they particularly liked this designated individual time with the coach.

The key to effective team performance is that each team member effectively performs differentiated (albeit interdependent) roles. Role understanding and acceptance are essential prerequisites to effective role performance. It is unlikely an athlete will perform well in a role he/she does not identify, understand, or accept as his/her own. Ownership is essential to personal responsibility. Athletes have commented that the roles process helped them understand what roles they should assume as their responsibility and the roles they should emphasize in practice and in games. At the same time, each athlete on the team realized there are times in competition an athlete will have to step up and just do what needs to be done.

In sum, the roles process requires a large investment of time from the head coach. However, role clarity is an essential ingredient for virtually all team sports. In my experience, the roles process has been effective in increasing role understanding and role acceptance in intercollegiate basketball, volleyball, and football teams. With sport-specific modifications to the Roles List, the same process likely could be used successfully to increase role clarity in other sports, as well.

The Importance of Team Values[1]

10

Many teams identify team goals and a team mission statement. However, an important prerequisite to strategic goal setting is clearly establishing team values. Values are underlying, guiding principles. Values are not objectives or outcomes. Rather, values are the principles that guide decisions and actions. The actions determine whether a team will reach its objectives or goals. Objectives or goals are the desired destination; values determine *how* the team gets there. Goal accomplishment requires maintaining perspective in terms of what the team is trying to accomplish and what is important in getting there. Values clarify the path to the goal. Shared team values are the foundation of a successful team and are critical to building trust among athletes and coaches. Values provide guidance to athletes and coaches for how they should respond to any situation, on or off the playing field.

Values commonly found in teams are achievement, challenge, communication, competition, cooperation, determination, fairness, family, fitness, fun, growth, honesty and integrity, individualism, learning, morality, high-level performance, pride, relationships, respect, responsibility, risk, security, timeliness, teamwork, uniqueness, and winning. There are many others. No particular value is more important than any other in an absolute sense. The relative importance of any value is specific to a given team and is determined by the goals, strategy, and philosophy of that team.

Because a team may have a number of values, at times there will be conflicting values. Also, athletes may at times find their personal values in conflict with team values. For example, if the team values "team first" and an athlete's individual value is "personal achievement," there clearly will be times when these two values will be in conflict. Such conflicts are unavoidable. When the team has a good understanding of its priorities and shared values, it enables athletes to more effectively resolve these inevitable conflicts. Shared values increase perceived similarity among teammates and increase identification with the team; increased identification, in turn, makes team goals and values more salient than personal goals.

It is important that team members "buy in" to the values so that they truly are shared values. When the team has shared goals and shared values, each team member believes other team members are more likely to behave in accordance with these values (integrity) and more likely to care about goals and outcomes that are good for all team members. When team members believe that they personally gain when the team succeeds, it creates cooperative interdependence and the most effective team effort toward accomplishing team goals. Congruent, shared core values lead to trust. Team members trust that others on the team embrace the same goals (desired outcomes) and will act in accordance with team values to achieve those goals.

I have worked with NCAA Division I basketball and volleyball teams at three different universities to facilitate developing team values. Integrity, Respect (self and others), Responsibility, Hard Work, and Team First were values that were common across the teams. Other values such as Timeliness, Direct Communication, or Family reflected points of emphasis specific to a given team. Team values served to guide individual athletes in making decisions about team-related performance on and off the court, whether acting independently or interdependently. Shared values prove to be the cornerstone of effective team performance.

The exercise for this chapter describes a process for identifying team values. This process should take place in conjunction with identifying team goals and obtaining commitment to achieving those goals. This technique presents an approach to resolving discrepancies between conflicting individual values and team values as well as discrepancies between team values and individual player choices. The technique is effective at building consensus on shared team values and in identifying the priority of each value for the team. The process can result in shared core values, productive team norms, and trust among teammates. Other issues that may be addressed in additional team building sessions are: discrepancies between team values and the choices one makes; discrepancies between personal values and team values; and discrepancies between individual goals and team goals.

Exercise to Identify Team Values

This exercise will take you through a process to identify the values you believe are important for guiding the team to success.

Individual "Team Values"

Values are underlying, guiding principles. Values are not objectives. Rather, values are the principles that guide decisions and actions. It is these actions that determine whether or not your team will reach its objectives and goals. Objectives and goals are desired destinations; values determine *how* you get to those destinations. Shared team values are critical to building trust and cooperation among teammates.

Common values are achievement, challenge, communication, competition, cooperation, determination, diversity, fairness, family, fitness, freedom, fun, growth, honesty and integrity, individualism, learning, morality, productivity, quality, quantity, relationships, respect, responsibility, risk, security, task focus, timeliness, team first, teamwork, uniqueness, winning. There are many others.

Take some time to reflect on what is important to the success of your team. Identify five team values that you truly believe in and are committed to using to guide the team. (**Note:** These should be team-level values that are important to the team. These values may or may not overlap with your personal values.)

List the five team values you believe are critical to the success of the team.

(Each team member and coach should complete this independently. The values may be but do not need to be from the examples above.)

1. _____

2. _____

3. _____

4. _____

5. _____

Combining Individual "Team Values"

Using a chalkboard or other means of displaying results, go around the room and list all of the values identified by each team member and coach. Use tally marks to indicate when more than one individual identified the same value. As each person reveals a value, ask him/her to explain how that value will help the team accomplish the shared team goals. After all have indicated all of the values they identified, move the team toward consensus on shared values by identifying which values were most often identified, consolidating similar values, and discussing which values are most important for team success. Once the team has decided on five to seven team values, have each team member complete the Prioritize Team Values worksheet independently.

Prioritize Team Values

No particular value is more important than any other in an absolute sense. The relative importance of any value is determined by the objectives/goals, strategy, and philosophy of the team. Because a team may hold a number of values, at times there will be conflicting values. (For example, if the team values "team effort" and "individual achievement," there clearly will be times when these two values will be in conflict with each other.) Such conflicts are unavoidable. When the team has a good understanding of its values and priorities, it helps team members to better resolve these inevitable conflicts.

To help clarify priorities for team values, first list the five to seven values the team identified. Each team member should take 100 points and allocate them among the five to seven values to indicate the relative importance of each value to accomplishing team objectives. (Allocating more points to a value indicates a greater priority for that value.) The total number of points allocated should sum to 100.

Value	Points
1. _____	_____
2. _____	_____
3. _____	_____
4. _____	_____
5. _____	_____
6. _____	_____
7. _____	_____

Total = 100

The value weights can be determined mathematically (i.e., sum total points allocated, then rank order the values based on this sum). Alternatively, the total points can be summed, then a discussion held to reinforce which value should take precedence should two values be in conflict in a particular situation. If the team as a whole allocates a low number of points to a value, that value should be deleted from the list of important values.

Note

1 The information in this chapter is based on previous work by the author published as Shoenfelt, E. L. (2010). "Values added" teambuilding: A process to ensure understanding, acceptance, and commitment to team values. *Journal of Sport Psychology in Action*, *1,* 150–160. Copyright © Association for Applied Sport Psychology, www.appliedsportpsych.org, reprinted by permission of Taylor & Francis Ltd, http://www.tandfonline.com on behalf of the Association for Applied Sport Psychology.

Strategic Goal Setting for Teams

11

Team building is commonly used to identify team goals and a team mission. In Chapter 3, I identified the characteristics of effective goals. Clearly stated, specific, and difficult goals (if there is acceptance/commitment and understanding), will result in higher performance than will ambiguous, nonspecific, easily attainable goals, or no goals at all. This holds true at the individual, group, and organizational level. Strategic goal setting involves both outcome and process goals. A critical component of the goal-setting process is the strategic planning reflected by process goals. In strategic goal setting, we drill down the process goals to identify specific individual responsibilities and how they combine to accomplish outcome goals for team. That is, the coaches and players discuss specific roles, responsibilities, and levels of performance required by individual athletes and the team for the team to reach their overarching goals for the season. In addition, it is essential to gain commitment from individual athletes to take responsibility for roles and the level of performance required to accomplish the team goals.

A Strategic Team Goal-Setting Process

In this chapter, I describe the annual goal-setting process I use with intercollegiate teams (e.g., basketball, volleyball, softball, soccer) to help those teams identify team outcome goals as well as the requisite process goals that will help ensure the achievement of the outcome goals. A detailed example of this strategic goal-setting process is then described step by step.

In **Step 1**, team members and coaches individually identify potential personal (individual player) and team goals prior to a team meeting. Players are required to submit individual season goals to the coach before the meeting.

Step 2 is the goal-setting team meeting, which usually lasts for about two hours. In this meeting, the key principles of goal setting are explained. Team Outcome Goals are identified, which typically vary only slightly from season to season. These goals are edited and prioritized, and are limited to five to seven overarching goals. Next, Team Process Goals are identified. There is open discussion between the coaches and players that targets who on the team has primary responsibility for each process goal and the specific performance(s) required to accomplish the goal. Individual players are assigned specific responsibilities to increase role clarity and understanding. Each player personally commits to the individual responsibilities delineated in the process goals.

An important co-requisite to strategic goal setting is clearly establishing team values. Values are underlying, guiding principles. Values are not objectives or outcomes. Rather, values are the principles that guide decisions and actions. Chapter 10 of this book provides a process for developing team values. The last thing in the team meeting is to reinforce team values to players and coaches; the values then serve as a guide for how goals will be accomplished.

The particulars of the strategic planning vary from season to season depending on the skill mix of the players, characteristics of the competition, and the coach's priorities for the season. The outcome and process goals are recorded and revisited for each competition.

Step 3 involves keeping statistics and providing team and individual feedback relative to each process goal after every competition. Players receive individual feedback on each of their responsibilities.

Outcomes from Strategic Goal Setting

Strategic goals provide a roadmap to guide the team across the season. There are targeted outcomes for the team and individual athletes. The process goals serve as individual roles assigned and clarified for each athlete. Relevant statistics are targeted for the team and for individuals. These stats are charted for each competition and are used to provide feedback on a team and individual basis. This feedback enables individual personal responsibility and accountability.

Example of Strategic Goal Setting with an Intercollegiate Volleyball Team

Each year the volleyball team at Western Kentucky University (WKU) holds a team meeting to set strategic goals for the season. I facilitate the meeting, but having a sport psychologist present is not necessary for strategic goal setting to work. WKU Volleyball is a very successful program (e.g., 16 straight 25+ win seasons; 10 NCAA tournament appearances in the last 12 years; 29 All Region and 21 NCAA All American players; 9 Coach of the Year awards). The coaches and players attribute much of their success to having specific, strategic goals and players who are focused on fulfilling responsibilities to accomplish those goals.

Step 1: Identify Team Outcome Goals

Prior to the team meeting, players develop individual goals and team goals and turn both sets of goals in to the coach. In the meeting, the sport psychologist provides a brief tutorial on goal setting highlighting these points:

- Goals must be understood and accepted.
- Goals should be specific and challenging, but realistic.
- Goals should be measurable.

- Outcome goals are long term and identify a destination.
- Process goals identify HOW to achieve the outcome goals.

The players and coaches hold an open discussion in which they indicate what they think the season goals for team should be. The sport psychologist records all nominated goals on the white board. Coaches let players speak first; coaches comment when asked by players or when they feel it is needed. Sophomores, juniors, and seniors have been through the process previously. Typically, the seniors and juniors take the lead in identifying goals and responding to questions of why a given goal is important. Players ask the coach when they want clarification if a goal is realistic or should be a priority this season. The nominated goals are edited, combined, and some goals are eliminated to result in five to seven outcome goals for the season.

The outcome goals identified are similar each year, but there is some variation depending on the composition of the team and the competition (schedule for the season). The team always includes an academic goal; for example, a Team GPA greater than or equal to 3.5. (The WKU Volleyball Team has been on the Academic Honor Roll of the American Volleyball Coaches Association (AVCA) for 11 consecutive seasons. Goal setting works for academics as well.) Typical outcome goals include:

- Get into the NCAA Tournament.
- Win conference tournament.
- Get an at-large bid.
- Progress in the NCAA Tournament.
- Team GPA greater than or equal to 3.5.
- Be positive, mentally tough.

Step 2: Identify the Strategic Process Goals that will Lead to Outcome Goal Accomplishment

After the outcome goals have been identified, the strategic part of the session begins. Players and coaches identify and discuss the required process goals necessary to accomplish the outcome goals. For each process goal, specific player responsibilities are assigned. The discussion targets whether a given player is willing to accept responsibility and ensuring that she will be held accountable for fulfilling each responsibility through personal responsibility and teammates holding her accountable. The strategic part is identifying process goals to support the outcome goals as well as the key players for each process goal.

An example of the strategic process goals for the outcome goal of "Progressing in NCAA Tournament" and the intermediate outcome goals of "Making the NCAA Tournament" and "Winning the Conference Tournament" include **identifying specific team statistics and WHO is responsible** for every role, including the following.

- Serving – Identify six great servers: Greater than or equal to 50% point scored percentage; less than or equal to 10% error percentage.
- Passing – Greater than 2.2 average rating for each passer.
- Hitting – Hitting percentage greater than .300; hitting percentage greater than opponent percentage; #1 hitting percentage in the conference.
- Blocking – Greater than or equal to 2.4 blocks per set.
- Stops – 12 stops per set; 2 stops per player.

Accomplishing the outcome goal of "Making the NCAA Tournament Through an At-large Bid" is largely determined by the pre-conference season win/loss record. Thus, identifying the strategic process goals for this outcome goal involves **identifying pre-conference match wins and losses**. The coach intentionally schedules a very tough pre-conference season so that, if the team performs well, it will be in a position to get an at-large bid. The preseason matches are listed on the white board and the coach identifies for each match whether WKU is expected to win, lose, or tie. WKU must win all matches they are expected to win, to win most of the matches that are expected ties, and they need to upset some of the teams they are expected to lose to. Thus, the team can reasonably identify the number of wins necessary to get an at-large bid to the NCAA tournament and the team knows which matches are critical to win. Although one might expect it is the upset matches that are most important, in reality there is more pressure to win the matches WKU is expected to win. A loss in one of these matches will likely foil an at-large bid. Thus, a typical process goal for pre-conference season is a "Record of 13 – 3 or better."

The Role of Team Values. After the strategic process goals are discussed and responsibilities assigned, the team values are reinforced. The team values are posted on the locker room wall and frequently are printed on practice t-shirts. Each team member is asked to write down the team values without looking at the posting on the wall. Next, I ask for a show of hands who got one, two, three, four, five, or all six team values. Then players as a group are asked to orally identify the six values. Values cannot guide behavior if the values are not known. Team values provide additional guidance on strategy. Values indicate **how** each player should respond in any situation. Upper classmen virtually always know all of the team values. Freshmen very quickly learn that the values are important and make a point of learning them.

Step 3: Provide Individual and Team Feedback and Hold Players Accountable

Statistics are kept for the key performances identified in the strategic process goals. After each match, players are eager to hear the statistics and value meeting their individual and team goal responsibilities. The importance players place on the strategic goals is illustrated by this quote to the press by a WKU senior outside hitter. "We sit down every year and we have a whole session where we jot down goals. We always have our big outcome goals and we always have process goals. Our process goals are how we're going to accomplish those outcome goals. A lot of our outcome goals are putting ourselves in position for an at-large bid. We want to be NCAA bound."

Conclusion

Strategic goal setting provides targeted outcomes for team and individuals by identifying and assigning team and individual responsibilities. This process results in role clarity, understanding, and acceptance. The statistics charted for each competition enable feedback on a team and individual basis, which leads to individual responsibility and accountability. The in-depth discussion during the goal-setting process ensures a common understanding between coaches and players on the road map to guide the team to success across the season.

Preparing for the Big Event

12

Here we are at the final chapter of the book, Preparing for the Big Event. Exactly what constitutes the Big Event will differ depending on your level of competition and your sport. The Big Event may range, for example, from getting your first start in a youth sport game to competing in the Olympics, and everything in between. The Big Event is a competition that is important to you. This chapter will help you reach your peak at the right time and to deal with the inevitable competitive anxiety most athletes feel as the Big Event approaches.

Before it is time for the Big Event, there is a lot of work to do. Most athletes find it difficult to maintain motivation for demanding practices throughout the season. Accordingly, the first topic in Preparing for the Big Event is staying strong throughout the season.

Maintaining Motivation: Staying Strong through the Mid-Season Drudgery

As teams cycle through the first half of their conference/district season, it is common to find athletes (and coaches) feeling the full effect of the grind of practices, competition, and travel. This time of the season may not be as stimulating as the first part of the season when everyone is fresh and excited to be back to practicing and back in the sport, or toward the end of the season when the conference tournament is approaching and everyone is hyped to play well. For some sports, this mid-season drudgery occurs about the time athletes return from a holiday break; the student-athlete has new academic responsibilities as well as team responsibilities.

There is a basic formula used in performance psychology to understand what factors impact performance:

$$\text{PERFORMANCE} = \text{ABILITY} \times \text{MOTIVATION} - (\text{SITUATIONAL CONSTRAINTS})$$

Ability refers to all of the sport specific skills you and your team members have (e.g., passing, shooting, serving, etc.) and as well as individual and team attributes/abilities (e.g., height, strength, speed, depth on the bench, etc.). **Motivation** refers to individual and team attitudes, beliefs, commitment, determination, effort, focus, etc. To a certain extent, ability and motivation are compensatory. That is, one who lacks ability can make up for it through additional effort. A highly skilled but unmotivated athlete may not outperform his less skilled teammates. It is important for any team, but especially important for "underdog" teams that have been performing well because of motivational factors, to maintain motivation throughout the course of the season. It can be difficult to maintain intensity, but it is necessary if the team wants to be successful. In competitive conferences/divisions/ districts where teams are close in ability, it is motivation (i.e., mental skills) that makes the difference in winning or losing.

I worked with swimmer Claire Donahue to help her prepare for the Olympic Trials and the Olympic Games. At the Olympic Trials, there were 160+ women competing for the two spots on the US Olympic Swim Team in her event. Claire's practice and preparation were different than for many sports because Claire had to prepare for several years to compete only three times (i.e., the prelims, the semis, and the finals) in a period of only two days at the Trials. One of my key contributions to her preparation was to help her stay motivated while she trained for four to six hours a day, six days a week, for more than a year. These were grueling practices. It was by focusing on what she dreamed of accomplishing and daily determination that sustained her during her practices. Her effort and commitment paid off as she earned a place on the US Olympic Swim Team and a gold medal in the 2012 Olympics.

Most athletes realize they need to give 100% every competition for the individual athlete and/or the team to perform well. What may not be recognized is that the way to ensure each athlete *can* give 100% in every competition is to work harder in practice than is needed to win in competition. Elite athletes know that a key to winning is to put forth so much effort in practice that competition seems easy by comparison. Can you say the same for yourself? That is, can you honestly say that you work so hard in practice that it is easy to give 100% in every competition? If not, then you and each member of your team need to make a conscious decision whether or not you are willing to do what it takes to make you and your team the best they can be. This determined, intentional practice is the way to maximize the ability and the accomplishments of you and your team.

Exercise 12.1: Work Today to Achieve Your Dream

Have each athlete on the team respond in writing to each question that follows. This can be done in a team meeting prior to practice. Athletes should then share their answers with the team. (Have each athlete respond to the first question, then each athlete respond to the second question, etc. You can ensure this progression by writing one question at a time on a white board.)

1. What can I do TODAY to ensure that my dream comes true?
2. What can I do to ensure I have done absolutely everything I could have done to achieve my goal of _____ [athletes fill in blank with individual and/or team goal]?
3. Am I willing to work 100% today – because today may make a difference in whether or not I/we accomplish my/our goal?

4. Perspective – Keep your eye on the prize. What is the ultimate goal and is it worth working hard today? If I knew that going 100% today in practice would mean the difference between succeeding and failing to accomplish my goal, how hard would I work in practice?

Athletes' written responses can be taped to their lockers to remind them that to be successful, good effort is required every day.

Mental Skills: Pre-Competition Routine

Now we move into mental skills for the Big Event. First is the pre-competition routine, followed by dealing with the distractions in the context of the Big Event, building confidence specifically for the Big Event and, finally, using summary sheets in preparation for the event.

In Chapter 8, I discussed the importance of routines for executing performance skills. Routines also are important for preparing for competition. Many athletes have a pre-competition routine that begins well before the competition arrives. For example, athletes may use intentional structured imagery to rehearse arriving at the competition venue, warming up, preparing to compete, competing, and performing well. In some sports (e.g. running, swimming), the pre-competition routine may involve tapering; that is, reducing practice time and exertion for several days prior to a big competition. Sleep is critical for optimal performance. Many athletes include going to bed early the night before a competition as an essential component of their routine. Proper nutrition is key; athletes should plan meals and snacks to ensure they have the nutritional energy to compete well. Most athletes have a written checklist of the equipment they need to pack and transport to the competition. This lists helps to ensure the athlete does not forget a key piece of equipment (e.g., shoes, socks, glove, goggles, etc.). The checklist should include spare equipment if it is common for a given piece of equipment to fail or get lost (e.g., swim caps tear; tennis rackets break strings).

As the actual competition draws near, an athlete's routine may include listening to music to psych up or calm down, stretching, warming up, and using imagery to focus on the keys to performance in the competition. The specific routine that is best for each athlete is determined by their sport and their individual characteristics. Athletes should check with their coach to see if s/he has suggestions for improving any pre-competition routine.

Finally, athletes need to "Expect the unexpected." This phrase means that, in any competition, something is likely to go wrong. If we recognize that we have the mental skills to deal with most unexpected situations, we will rise to the challenge and handle the difficult situation well. In Chapter 2 you learned the importance of responding to challenges in a positive manner, focusing on your circle of control and what you can do in a tough situation. Your mental skills provide confidence that you can handle difficult situations. In Chapter 5 you learned to anticipate problems and how to prepare for a challenging situation – that is, by identifying and developing positive responses to "What ifs?" Once you have developed responses to the rational "What Ifs?" and are comfortable that you can deal with them, another positive step is "Wait to worry" – that is, don't stress out about things that might happen; wait to deal with them **if/when** they do happen. The key is to trust the mental skills now in your toolbox and the resilience you have developed, and to adjust and adapt to the situation before you.

Mental Skills: The (Distracting) Role of Context

Even successful athletes frequently feel anxious about performing in the big game, the big match, or some other high-level competition. One reason for this anxiety is that the athlete is distracted by the **context** of the performance. That is, the performance requirements for the competition are exactly the same as they have been leading up to the big game (i.e., the court or field is exactly the same size; the ball is the same size, shape, and weight; the net is the same height; etc.), but the context in which the competition is occurring has changed. This competition is more important than a regular season match or game because of the consequences of the outcome. Perhaps it is a single elimination competition and it is either "do or die," or it is the final of a tournament and winning would bring glory and recognition to the athlete and/or team.

Athletes need to learn to use attentional focus to block out distractions and to focus on the task(s) they need to perform. This attentional focusing includes blocking out both the physical distractions and mental distractions before and during competition (e.g., competing athletes staying in the same hotel, a larger arena, bigger crowds, press questions and statements, thinking about outcomes such as winning or losing, etc.). Athletes need to focus on the process (i.e., performance on the court or field) rather than the context or the outcome (i.e., winning or losing, advancing to the next round). Athletes should focus on the "3 Ps" (the Present Positive Performance) – that is, focus on the current moment and what they need to do on the court or on the field to perform well to win the current point. Fortunately, for athletes that have made it to this level of competition, it is likely they have performed their sport well hundreds of times before. The only thing different now is the context; the athlete simply needs to perform his/her sport as s/he has successfully done many, many times before. If the athlete can focus on the positive performance s/he needs to accomplish rather than the distractions of context, s/he greatly increases his/her chance of being successful.

To illustrate the effect context can have on performance, consider the balance beam on which a gymnast performs complicated routines. If we place that balance beam on the floor, most of us would have no trouble walking across the beam without falling. It is a relatively simple task. Now, if we take the very same balance beam and raise it 6 feet off the ground, most of us would have difficulty walking across the beam without falling. Why? Because we are no longer focused on the simple task of walking the beam; we are now focused on the distance between the beam and the floor – that is, the context in which we are performing the task. The task of walking the beam has not changed, but mentally we made the task far more difficult and increased our anxiety by focusing on the distraction of the space between the beam and the floor. It also is likely that we now are distracted by negative self-talk focused on outcomes (e.g., What if I fall? Will I look foolish if I fall? What if I cannot be successful?). We are much more likely to be successful walking the beam if we focus on the task, block out the distractions, and use positive self-talk. Likewise, an athlete in a big competition is much more likely to be successful if s/he blocks out the distractions of the context and focuses on the task performance that s/he has performed successfully many times before.

Exercise 12.2: Setting Aside Distractions

This exercise may be used a day before the competition or the day of the competition. Coaches and athletes each should have two large index cards and a marker to write with. On one card, write the word "DISTRACTIONS." On this card, write down every distraction, everything you are concerned about for the upcoming competition; everything you are thinking about other than what you are going to do on the court/field/course. Distractions might include: competing athletes staying in the same hotel, a larger arena, bigger crowds, press questions and statements, thinking about outcomes such as winning or losing, family and friends who are asking for time and will be in the stands, an upcoming test, boyfriend or girlfriend issues, etc.

On the other card, write the word "FOCUS." On this card, write down what you need to do on the court/field/course. Focus on the "3 Ps" (the Present Positive Performance). Include your affirmation statements/performance cues – the keys to your performing well. You know what your role is during competition – what your coaches and teammates need you to do on the court/field/course. Write it down on the card. Focus points should include the tasks you are responsible for during competition. Examples for basketball might include rebounding, blocking out, floor leader, passing, shooting, communicating, etc. Examples for volleyball might include hitting, setting, passing, serving, reading offense, etc. Examples for golf might include shot routine, error management, reading greens, etc. Examples for baseball might include maintaining focus in the field, base running, hitting, etc.

Next, crumble up the Distraction card and put it in the bottom of your locker (or somewhere you won't readily see it). Leave the distractions there until the competition is over. Then, once the competition is over, if you want to, you can retrieve the distractions or you may leave them behind for good. Keep the Focus card in a prominent place where you will readily see it (e.g., taped to your locker or mirror, etc.). Leave the distractions in the locker, but take the focus points with you out on the court/field/course.

Other techniques can be incorporated to reinforce the idea of leaving distractions behind, for example:

- Prior to the competition, athletes can use slow deep breathing to relax and calm their minds. Then they can close their eyes and focus on their roles in the competition.
- When a volleyball team lines up for introductions immediately prior to the start of the match, instead of waving "hello" to the crowd, they can use the same wave to "wave goodbye" to distractions and at that point, focus only on performance.

You can think of other pre-competition points where you can leave distractions behind and fully focus on the task at hand.

Mental Skills: The Four Pillars of Confidence

Successful athletes are confident. Confidence is developed over time through a combination of positive thinking and success experiences. Confident athletes consistently use constructive thinking to focus on and benefit from their successes and to minimize errors and losses. Confidence enables us to trust our performance.

Competition involves setbacks, obstacles, and disappointments; the successful athlete must respond optimistically (i.e., focus on what I *can do*) rather than focusing on the negative (i.e., what is wrong or undesirable) to remain confident and to perform well. Errors should be viewed as an exception to your typical good performance; that is, the error reflects only one shot, one play, or one game. Successful performance should be expected and should be thought of as representative of your actual ability. This mind set will help build resilience; that is, the ability to overcome challenges, adapt in the face of adversity, and quickly recover from setbacks and difficulties. Confidence in your ability to perform well on a given task or in a specific situation such as a game, match, or tournament is referred to as self-efficacy. Those with high self-efficacy persist longer in the face of challenges, set higher goals, and attain higher levels of performance.

There are four primary sources of confidence: success experiences, vicarious experience, verbal persuasion, and physical arousal. Each of these four pillars of confidence contributes to positive self-talk that will build and maintain confidence.

The first pillar is previous success. As an athlete, you have experienced success many times, whether this season or in a previous season. Focus on these successes. Your success experiences may have occurred in practice as you mastered a new skill or improved upon a skill learned long ago, or the successes may have occurred in competition. Think of competitions where you performed your best. Coaches should help to ensure athletes experience success by providing challenges appropriate to the athlete's skill level. As the athlete develops greater skill, s/he will be successful in even more challenging situations.

The second pillar of confidence is vicarious experiences of success. Vicarious success refers to feeling successful or experiencing success through the actions of others. It can take two forms.

First, think of other successful athletes in your sport that you admire. Use these athletes as your model to learn success by observing how they attained success. It is especially effective for building confidence if you know of the obstacles and difficulties these athletes overcame to attain success. Likewise, if these athletes are similar to you in terms of a range of personal characteristics that may include age, gender, body build, skill level, etc., the model may be more effective in building confidence. If these athletes can be successful, then you should be confident that you too can be successful.

The second form of learning confidence vicariously is modeling your own success. Create a highlight video of your best performances. Watch the video again and again. Seeing yourself succeed will build confidence that you can succeed again. In addition, using imagery to see yourself succeed in a difficult situation will help build confidence.

The third pillar of confidence is verbal persuasion. Think of positive feedback you have received about your performance. Verbal persuasion is more effective at building confidence if it comes from a credible source with expertise in your sport (e.g., your coach, your teammate, sports writers, etc.). If these individuals that know the sport believe you can be successful, then you too should believe that you will be successful. Positive self-talk is important because what you tell yourself about your performance can be an important source of confidence. Negative self-talk can decrease confidence and is detrimental to performance.

The fourth pillar of confidence is physiological arousal. If you are calm, cool, collected, and ready to compete, your body is signaling confidence. If, on the other hand, you are anxious with sweaty palms and a dry mouth, your body is signaling nervousness and a lack of confidence. Learning to control physiological arousal through relaxation techniques is an effective way to build confidence. When you are relaxed and ready to compete, you will feel more confident.

In sum, there are a number of factors that influence an athlete's confidence. It is important for the athlete to focus on all four pillars of confidence. Using positive self-talk to emphasize successes and to minimize any errors helps to ensure the athlete will be confident of his/her ability to overcome inevitable obstacles and setbacks during competition. The exercise below can be completed prior to an important competition to ensure the athlete is focusing on the four pillars of confidence.

Exercise 12.3: Building Confidence

Build Confidence for (event) _____

Name: _____

What are reasons you should succeed? What should you list?

1. Think in terms of **success(es) you have had in the same or similar events** – list those.
2. Think in terms of all of the **practices where you were able to perform this event successfully** – list those.
3. Think in terms of the **imagery/visualization where you have seen yourself succeed** many times in the very event you are considering – list that. That is, *I have seen myself successfully perform this event a hundred times.*
4. Think in terms of significant **others with expertise in the event who have expressed confidence** in your ability to succeed (e.g., your coach, your teammates, etc.) – list each of those. They know what they are talking about and they have confidence in you.
5. Think in terms of **others who have characteristics in common with you who have succeeded** in this event (e.g., teammates, even competitors with whom you share similarities) – list those. That is, *if _____ can be successful in this event, then I can too because we are similar.*
6. Think in terms of your **imagery/visualization where you saw yourself calm, cool, and collected and ready to compete in this event** (i.e., using relaxation to gain the optimal level of arousal). That is, you are physically ready to compete – list that.
7. Think in terms of the many **other qualities that you have that help you perform well** in this event – list that.
8. Think in terms of **any other reason** that should help you succeed in this event – list those reasons.

List 10 reasons you should succeed.

1. _____
2. _____
3. _____
4. _____
5. _____
6. _____
7. _____
8. _____
9. _____
10. _____

This list will help you focus on the positive reasons you should perform well. Remember that champion athletes focus on their successes. They think of their strengths and successes as typical and characteristic of their performance. They think of errors or poor performances as atypical and as exceptions to their typically good performance.

Summary Sheets

If you have been working hard to develop mental skills, it may be helpful to develop a summary sheet that reminds you of the different mental skills in your toolbox and the time and place to use them. Below, I share two examples (summary sheets 12.1 and 12.2). One is the complex grid sheet Claire Donahue used to prepare for the Olympic Swim Trials and, subsequently, the 2012 Olympics. The second is simpler; it is a motivational sheet I prepared for our volleyball team members as they were headed to the NCAA tournament. The sheet captures the essence of what each athlete needs to focus on for the team to be successful. You may be able to adapt one of these two sheets or you may come up with one of your own.

Summary Sheet 12.1

CLAIRE DONAHUE: MENTAL TOUGHNESS GUIDE				
Performance Component	**Objective for Component**	**Goal**	**Performance Cues**	**Performance Thought / Performance Cue**
Start/Reaction Time	Fast/Strength – Keep as is			
1st Underwaters	9/10 UW's	# of kicks / uw's	Yes	Push 8, Push 9 – Acceleration Time
1st 50 Fast	Fast/Strength – Keep as is			Attack Strong
1st Wall	Strong to the Wall	# times used cues	Yes	See the wall; Give it your all; Knees Up
2nd Underwaters	8/9 UW's	# of kicks / uw's	Yes	Push 8, Push 9 – Acceleration Time
Finish Strong	Fast Final 50		Yes	Elbows, Press, Kick Pain to Attain
PRACTICE				
4 Walls/8 Walls				
Motivation	Stay Motivated			Use Worksheets
MENTAL SKILLS				
Positive Self-Talk	Use / Track Positive Self-talk			3 Ps: Present Positive Performance
Visualization	Track 3 weeks before Big Event	7 days/wk		
Confidence Sheets	Review			
Relaxation	Use when anxious			1-Breath Relaxation (3 times)

Summary Sheet 12.2

We Are Here To Compete!

"BRING IT!"
Every point of every set of every match.

CONTROL THE CONTROLLABLES:

→ How YOU Respond
→ Arousal/Relaxation
→ Attention/Focus

Focus on the "3 Ps" – Present Positive Performance

- Be fully focused and compete every point of every set of every match.
- Don't worry about the past (any mistake you make is now history – you cannot change it) – or – the future (whether you win or lose is dependent on how you play right now). The point of power is right now.
- The most important point is the current one. Take care of every point and you will win the set; if you win the sets, you will win the match. Take care of business one point at a time.
- Worry not whether you will win or lose – but what you need to do right now.

Additional Exercises and Techniques

In this section I offer two additional exercises for preparing for the Big Event. The first (the team exercise) intentionally creates performance anxiety to provide perspective. The second (a technique for developing the mindset of a champion) compiles relevant mental skills for preparing for the competition.

(Team) Exercise 12.4: Singing the Star Spangled Banner

In this exercise, the athlete will be made to feel anxious. Psychologists make an important distinction between anxiety and fear. Fear is apprehension in response to a real and present danger. Anxiety is generalized dread and apprehension without a realistic cause. Competitive anxiety is feeling anxious about competing even though the athlete has prepared and is performing the same skills s/he has performed many times before. This exercise is intended to create anxiety and then demonstrate several lessons about understanding and controlling anxiety.

Most people are anxious about public speaking; however, most are even more are anxious about singing individually in public. In this exercise, athletes are told they will individually be singing a line of the Star Spangled Banner aloud in front of a group. The group typically consists of teammates who also are participating in the exercise or it may be a group of fans. Some athletes may be comfortable with singing aloud in a semi-public setting, but most are not. With small teams, do this exercise as a team. With larger teams, the team may need to break into groups. Explain to the team that the team will stand up, then each athlete individually will sing one line of the Star Spangled Banner. Pass out the words to the song and have athletes stand.

The Star Spangled Banner

Oh, say can you see
By the dawn's early light
What so proudly we hailed
By the twilight's last gleaming?
Whose broad stripes and bright stars
Through the perilous flight
O'er the ramparts we watched
Were so gallantly streaming

And the rocket's red glare,
The bombs bursting in air
Gave proof through the night
That our flag was still there.
Oh, say does that Star Spangled banner
yet wave
O'er the land of the free and the home of
the brave?

After having the athletes stand, "remember" something else you want to talk to them about. Tell them to sit for a minute, then present some other information. Do this several times: have them stand, then relieve them. Ask how many are anxious about singing? (In some cases, I have spread this over a couple of team meetings on consecutive days at a tournament.)

Indicate to team members they really are going to sing this time.

1. Take deep breaths to create a calm mind. Breathe in slowly, breathe out slowly.
2. Use positive self-talk to think about your line and how you are going to sing it.
3. Now ask: "Who is anxious about singing? Why?" Typical responses include: *not confident; not a good singer; I don't sing solo very often or not at all; others will ridicule me; I will be embarrassed.*
4. Follow up with: "Who is a pretty good singer? What if we let just those athletes sing the lines?"
5. Finally, suggest: "What if we sing the lines as a group?"
6. Have just those athletes who are comfortable sing (either individually or as a team) – or – have the team sing Happy Birthday to an athlete who has a recent or upcoming birthday.

Lessons Learned

What are the "Take Aways" from this Team Exercise? Consider the following.

- You are not competing alone – the whole team will be out on the court/field. You don't have to do everything yourself. This is why you have teammates. Each person has a role. (Fortunately, singing is not likely any athlete's role during competition.)
- In this competition, you are not being asked to do anything other than what you have done hundreds of times before, and done it well. You have a role on the team; you bring a unique skill set to the team. If a certain skill is not your strength (e.g., singing or a sport related skill), it is likely someone else on the team has that strength. You bring something different, your special strengths to the team. With all team members playing together, with everyone bringing their strengths and fulfilling their role on the team, we have the whole package.
- You don't have to be perfect; just good enough to get the job done. You were able to sing the Star Spangled Banner – you got the job done. An ugly win is still a win and counts the same as a pretty win.
- If you sang Happy Birthday as a group, why was this so much easier than singing the Star Spangled Banner? It is because you have sung it many times (like the skills you will perform in the competition)? Is it because the whole team was singing together (just as the team will be competing together)?
- **Perspective 1.** Did you have realistic concerns about singing or was it just anxiety? Anxiety is nervousness and/or apprehension without an identifiable or realistic cause. Fear is realistic apprehension to a real danger. Was there something to fear? Not really. Worst-case scenario, you might be a little embarrassed – but, what does that really matter? In the whole scheme of things, it doesn't. There is nothing to fear now or in the upcoming competition. If you are anxious, you can control that through relaxation (i.e., control of physiological arousal) and positive self-talk. Focus on the "3 Ps": Present Positive Performance and focus on one play at a time.
- **Perspective 2.** Really, how important is it if you don't sing well? (You are not a men's/women's choir.) How does it compare to something that really is awful? Maintain perspective on what is really important. Beware of awfulizing – how does being a bit anxious and perhaps a bit embarrassed compare to something really awful? It does not at all compare. Did you have realistic concerns or anxiety? This competition is not something you should be anxious about. You should be pleased and excited that you have made it this far. All you have to do is exactly what you have done a hundred times – exactly what got you here. (See the discussion of perspective in Chapter 2 on Self-Talk.)

In sum, the "big" competition requires only that you do what you have done many times before and have done well. You, along with your teammates, bring the total package to the competition. If each team member fulfills his/her role responsibilities, the team will do well. All you have to do is bring your strengths and count on your teammates to do the same. You don't have to be perfect to get the job done; an ugly win is still a win. Keep perspective. There is nothing to fear. If you feel anxious, control the anxiety through relaxation and positive self-talk. Interpret any negative energy in a positive way, as excitement rather than anxiety.

Exercise 12.5: Develop the Mindset of a Champion

This exercise summarizes key mental skills likely to come into play in preparing for the Big Event. Adapt the content so that it works for you.

1. The "3 Ps": Present Positive Performance
    a. **Present** – focus on the present – what you can do now. The only point of impact is now; you can't change the past; you can't impact the future – except through what you do right now to prepare for your best performance (e.g., relax, imagery, confidence). The power is in the present. Forget about past poor performance and focus on what you need to do right now.
    b. **Positive** – focus on what you want to accomplish, not what you are trying to avoid. What is the positive desired performance you want to execute right now?
    c. **Performance** – focus on the skill you need to execute at this moment. Not the outcome (win or lose). Focus on what you need to do right now to win – focus on your performance and the process that will achieve the desired outcome.
2. Relax – Deep Breath Relaxation
    a. Inhale to a slow count of three; hold it for a count to three; exhale to a slow count of three. Repeat three times.
    b. **Mind–Body Connection** – when the body tenses up, it sends a message to the mind that you are nervous – maybe you cannot handle the situation. On the other hand, when you relax, it sends a message to the mind that, yes, you were a little anxious, but you controlled it and are now calm, cool, in control, and ready to compete.
3. Context – The Role of Context
    a. Review the balance beam example of the distracting role of context (see earlier in this chapter).
    b. **Ignore context and focus on your task performance**
        i. Focus on Task (what you do) vs. Context (e.g., who else, what, when, where).
        ii. Focus on Task vs. What Ifs.
        iii. Focus on Task (the positive performance you want to happen) vs. Negatives (what you want to avoid).
4. Confidence
    a. Refer to Exercise 12.3: Building Confidence
        i. Complete the confidence exercise earlier in this chapter.
        ii. In this competition, it is the same distance, same equipment, same court or field, and same task.
    b. Use positive self-talk.
5. Adapt and Adjust
    a. Recognize and accept that there will be things that don't go as planned.
    b. Have confidence in yourself, your teammates, and your coaches that you can adapt and adjust. Trust your coaches, trust your teammates, and trust yourself.
    c. Find a way to win!
6. Bring your A game
    a. Execute to the best of your ability.
    b. Enjoy the experience. You have worked hard to get here, so make the most of the moment.

Example of Developing the Mindset of a Champion

The example that follows is the Mindset of a Champion sheet Claire Donahue used to prepare for (and excel at) the US Olympic Swim Trials.

Claire Donahue
Olympic Trials: The Mindset of a Champion

When you get nervous ...

1. Ask yourself "Is this a realistic concern?" – if not, use mental skills and techniques to control the nervousness (i.e., relaxing breaths, positive self-talk, affirmation statements, reasons to feel confident, DREAM sheet). If it is a realistic concern, see Coach or Betsy.
2. Convert the nervousness into positive energy – excitement, psyching up for performance, etc.
3. Prepare in advance for how you should react to [others, media, in the arena]:
    a. things you see
    b. things you hear
    c. things others may do.
    Prepare so that you control your response – you are positive and confident – use positive self-talk and/or visualization.

Claire is fully prepared and ready to swim!
Remember that you have done EVERYTHING you need to do to be ready – you are ready!

Use mental skills to deal with context. Your task now is exactly the same as what you have been doing very successfully all year – many, many times. The 100 meters is exactly the same length as the other 100-meter races. The only thing different is the context. Control your reaction to the context and the task is simply swimming 100 meters like you have done hundreds of times. You don't have to do anything different and you don't have to do it perfectly – swim your race. Look at the pool – see a 50-meter pool and focus on the task and the "3 Ps." Just do what you know you can do and have done very well many times ... swim your race.

> **Example from Basketball.** A basketball player should be able to make a free throw with his/her eyes closed. It is the same shot, the same distance, on every basketball court. But, in big games, athletes get nervous because of the context. When they block out the distractions and stay fully focused on the task – the free throw (think "3 Ps" here) – they can make the shot easily.
>
> **Example from gymnastics – walking a balance beam.** If the beam is on the ground, you and I can easily walk the length of the beam; but if you raise the beam 6 feet off the ground, suddenly we have trouble. The task is exactly the same, but we are attending to the context instead of focusing fully on the task. Focus on the "3 Ps", not the context, not the outcome and certainly not "What if I fall?"

I Had the Time of My Life ...

Swimming in the Olympic Trials is an exciting opportunity and one that few swimmers get to do – so enjoy it!

Try to have a perspective on the trials as something that you will cherish for the rest of your life. When your kids ask you what it was like trying out for the Olympics, what do you want to be able to tell them? Let that guide your positive outlook on the whole week.

Think of how you feel about other happy, exciting occasions (e.g., Christmas with your family or your birthday), and treat the trials like that. When you are anticipating it, you are excited and looking forward to it. When the day comes, you are eager and excited (not nervous).

Build good memories of your Olympic Trials experience by using positive emotions.

"I am good enough that I don't have to be perfect to get in." Strive for excellence, not perfection. Things can go wrong or not as expected and you can still have a great swim.

Stay focused on the present. What can you do today/right now to ensure you have a great swim in the finals?

- Use relaxation breathing to stay physically relaxed.
- Use positive visualization to overcome any obstacles you are concerned about.
- Incorporate the nuances you know about this pool into your visualization.
- Use positive self-talk when you talk to yourself/think about any and every aspect of the competition.
- Use performance thoughts (See the wall ..., push ..., stay strong ..., etc.).
- Enjoy being here!

Control how you respond. When you feel nervous, ask yourself: "Am I controlling the controllables?" (i.e., using all of the mental skills to control how you respond, following Coach's guidance for prep, etc.). If the answer is yes, then you are doing exactly what you should be doing. So, feel confident and prepared.

Part IV

Epilogue

Epilogue

The mental skills in this book, if practiced and used in competition, will help ensure that you achieve your performance potential. Reaching your potential is more than just the outcome of a competition; it also is about the journey. At the end of the season, only one team/athlete goes home a winner. However, everyone can have a positive experience competing. Success requires self-discipline and hard work. The self-management skills that help you prepare to compete in sport are life skills that will help you in other endeavors, as well. It is my sincere hope that you appreciate the journey as much as you enjoy competing and performing well. Work hard, have fun, and enjoy your sport activities!

Index

accountability 4, 125, 133–5
affirmation statements 11, 14–15, 23–32, 48, 80–1, 109, 140, 151; *see also* performance cue
after action review 73, 75
attention 12–13, 36, 40, 85–8, 93–9, 108, 139, 146; attentional space 12, 97, 99
anxiety *see* competitive anxiety; performance anxiety
automaticity 5, 56, 96–9, 101–3, 105, 107, 109–10; perfect practice 98, 100; role of consistency 96–9; *see also* routines

big event: confidence for 138, 140–3, 150; defined 136; distracting context 138–40, 150–1; maintaining motivation 136–8; pre-competition routines 138–9
breathing *see* relaxation

closed skill 56, 89, 101–4, 110
commitment 113–14, 125, 128, 132, 137
competitive anxiety 5, 85–6, 136, 148; *see also* performance anxiety
concentration *see* focus
confidence 4–5, 9–11, 14, 55–8, 66, 71–4, 79, 85–7, 102–3, 105, 107, 138, 140–3, 150
consistency *see* automaticity; routines
context 5, 102, 108, 138–9, 150–1
continuous learning 72–8; *see also* problem solving
controllables 4, 9, 146, 152
cooperation 127, 129

distractions *see* big event; focus
dominant response 71, 99
downward spiral 9, 86

error-based learning 73–4
expect the unexpected 5, 72, 138

feedback 3, 41, 96, 133, 135; team feedback 135; *see also* goals; roles; strategic goal setting
focus 3–4, 9, 11–15, 17–22, 33–7, 41–2, 71, 74, 80, 85–8, 93–4, 97, 106–9, 137–44, 146, 149–52; appropriate/inappropriate 33–4, 86; breadth 13–14; 33–4; direction (internal *vs.* external) 13–14, 33–4; distractions 5, 12–15, 35–7, 78, 85, 92–5, 101–3, 105, 107–8, 138–40, 150–1
focus areas 15, 23–32, 43, 48, 49

goal orientation 41, 74; learning goal orientation 41; learning mindset 74; performance goal orientation 41
goals 4, 5, 18, 23, 32, 38, 40–54; effective goals checklist 47; feedback in relation to goals 40, 41, 44–6, 125, 133, 135; goal commitment 132; goal setting 42–7; goal setting-satisfaction paradox 42, 51–4; outcome goals 41, 43–6, 132–5

habit 10, 23, 42, 71, 99; *see also* automaticity
habituation 95

imagery 5, 10, 13, 42, 45, 49, 55–8, 70–1, 73, 80–1, 102–3, 105, 110, 138, 143, 150; arm as steel bar 68; basic senses 64; for confidence 57; for problem solving 57, 70–1; rating scale 58–63; ring on a string 69; sport specific 65–7; *see also* mental rehearsal; visualization
integrity 127–9

learned resourcefulness 72–4
learning 44–6, 55, 73–8, 96–9, 141–2, 149; from competition 75; learning mindset 74; from practice 75; three stages of 96, 98, 99; *see also* problem solving
listening 37, 98, 138; attentive listening 95

mental rehearsal 55–7, 69, 71, 102, 108; *see also* imagery; visualization
mental toughness 4–5, 73, 103, 145; *see also* confidence; resilience
mind body connection 4–5, 12, 14, 86, 150
mindfulness 85, 87, 93; habituation 95; listening 95; of a raisin 94; of our senses 93, 94
mindset of a champion 147, 150–1
motivation 136–8; defined 38; instrumentality theory 39; intrinsic *vs.* extrinsic 39–40; multiply determined 42; reinforcement theory 38–9; *see also* goals
muscle memory 55–6, 101–3, 105–17, 110; *see also* automaticity

negative self-talk 9–11, 14–17, 19–23, 25, 27, 29, 34, 64, 71, 79, 139, 141; awfulizing 9–10, 149

optimal level of arousal 85–7, 143; zone of 86

perfectionist 42, 51–4
performance anxiety 5, 55, 85, 87, 147–8; *see also* competitive anxiety
performance cue 11, 14, 20, 22–3, 31, 46, 48–9, 78, 79, 102–3, 105, 109–10, 140, 145; *see also* affirmation statement; performance thought
performance thought 102, 145; *see also* performance cue
perspective 10, 14, 42, 72–4, 95, 127, 138, 147, 149, 152; in imagery and visualization 54, 56, 70
physiological arousal: control of *see* optimal level of arousal; relaxation
positive self-talk 9–14, 16–23, 25, 27, 29, 31, 42–3, 46, 55, 71–4, 86, 139, 141–2, 148–52; self-talk journal 17; self-talk tracking 23–30
practice 3–5, 11, 14, 17, 18, 20, 31, 33, 35–6, 41–2, 45–6, 48–50, 72–3, 75–8, 81, 96–100, 102–3, 125–6, 136–8, 141, 143, 145, 155; consistent practice 96–7, 99; deliberate practice 3, 99; perfect practice 98, 100; through imagery 55–7, 66, 69, 71; *see also* routines
problem solving 5, 13, 57, 72–9; error management 73, 140; through imagery 57; *see also* continuous learning; learned resourcefulness; resilience
punishment 39

relaxation 5, 14, 55, 57, 71–3, 85–7, 89, 101, 102, 105, 108–9, 142–3, 145–6, 149–50, 152; breathing 20, 33, 67, 85–7, 89, 90, 93, 101–2, 105, 107–10, 140, 145, 148, 150, 152; tracking 90–2
resilience 4–5, 10, 72–4, 139, 141; adjust and adapt 72–3, 150
responsibility: personal responsibility 4, 114, 126–7, 129, 132–5
roles: role acceptance 114, 126, 135; role ambiguity 113–14; role clarity 113–14, 124, 126, 133, 135; role feedback 115, 118, 120; role grid 115–23; role understanding 113–14, 125–6, 133, 135, 138–9; roles process 113–15, 125–6
routines 5, 45, 56–7, 78, 81, 99–100, 101–4, 140; baseball 109; basketball 108; The Doer 101–5; 107–9; football 110; golf 105; pre-competition routine 138; pre-performance routine 101–2, 104, 107–10; post-performance routine 101, 106, 107

self-efficacy 39, 141
self-talk *see* positive self-talk; negative self-talk
serve thought 102, 107; *see also* performance cue
strategic goal setting 132–5; process goals 133–5; outcome goals 133
stress 4, 5, 72, 85–8, 97, 99, 103, 109–10, 113, 138
superstitions 103
swing thought 78, 105; *see also* performance cue

"3 Ps" 11–14, 34, 42, 107, 139–40, 146, 149–51; present positive performance 12–14, 19, 20, 42, 74, 139–40, 146, 149–50
trust: performance 10–11, 101–3, 105, 107, 109–10, 139, 140; teammates and coaches 80–1, 127–9, 150

values 40, 127–31, 133–5; individual/personal values 40, 127, 128–9; prioritize values 130–2; shared/team values 127, 128, 130, 133, 135
visualization 5, 12, 33, 45, 49, 55–8, 60, 62, 63, 66–71; *see also* imagery mental rehearsal

"what ifs" 79–81, 138, 150